CW01391091

SNAPREVISE

SnapRevise Text Guide:
Much Ado About Nothing
by William Shakespeare

Brynnie Rafe

InStudent Education UK Ltd owner of SnapRevise® trademark.
43 Priston Close, Worle, BS22 7FL, Weston-Super-Mare, United Kingdom

www.snaprevise.co.uk

Copyright © InStudent Publishing Pty Ltd 2024

All rights reserved. These notes are protected by copyright owned by InStudent Publishing Pty Ltd and you may not reproduce, disseminate, or communicate to the public the whole or a substantial part thereof except as permitted at law or with the prior written consent of InStudent Publishing Pty Ltd.

Title: Much Ado About Nothing by William Shakespeare Text Guide
ISBN: 978-1-917424-30-1

Published by InStudent Education UK Ltd CN 15550989 under licence from InStudent Publishing Pty Ltd.
ACN 624 188101

Disclaimer

No reliance on warranty. These SnapRevise materials are intended to supplement but are not intended to replace or to be any substitute for your regular school attendance, for referring to prescribed texts, or for your own note taking. You are responsible for following the appropriate syllabus, attending school classes, and maintaining good study practices. It is your responsibility to evaluate the accuracy of any information, opinions, and advice in these materials. Under no circumstance will InStudent Publishing Pty Ltd or InStudent Education UK Ltd ("Publishers"), their officers, agents, or employees be liable for any loss or damage caused by your use or reliance on these materials, including any adverse impact upon your performance in any academic subject as a result of your use or reliance on the materials. You accept that all information provided or made available by the Publishers is in the nature of general information and does not constitute advice. It is not guaranteed to be error-free and you should always independently verify any information, including through use of a professional teacher and other reliable resources. To the extent permissible at law, the Publishers expressly disclaim all warranties or guarantees of any kind, whether express or implied, including without limitation any warranties concerning the accuracy or content of information provided in these materials or other fitness for purpose. The Publishers shall not be liable for any direct, indirect, special, incidental, consequential or punitive damages of any kind. You agree to indemnify the Publishers, its officers, agents, and employees against any loss whatsoever by using these materials.

Preface

I've always been a voracious reader and an enthusiastic theatre-goer so it's not surprising that English subjects have always been my favourites. I think there's something special about Shakespeare though – I've always been fascinated by the almost unlimited capacity of his plays to be adapted and transformed in different productions: even a single line's meaning can be subtly altered in each iteration.

My first experience of *Much Ado About Nothing* was watching Joss Whedon's 2012 film adaptation on a rainy afternoon in an arthouse cinema in Hobart. While I tend to prefer tragedies, there's something incredibly captivating about Benedick and Beatrice's witty sparring – it's so much fun, and their eventual love match is built on equal intelligence and mutual trust. I still remember exactly how fierce Beatrice sounded when she said "Kill Claudio" – nearly 500 years later and it's still a show-stopping line.

Reading the play today, it's easy to spot lots of clichés: the sparring lovers, the badass, intelligent woman, the bumbling detectives – but for Shakespeare's audience, this was new. Without *Much Ado,* I think romcoms today might be very different, and almost certainly not as entertaining.

As with any Shakespeare, you might find reading the play a challenge at first – the humour can definitely be a bit obscure. However, *Much Ado's* resemblance to modern romcoms makes it more accessible than many of Shakespeare's other works and it's ultimately a joy to study.

— Brynnie Rafe

Contents

~ SnapRevise® ~

Section 1

Nutshell Summary

Our story begins in **Messina**. Leonato, the governor, and Beatrice, his niece, are waiting for Don Pedro, a prince, to return from a successful battle. A messenger informs them that Don Pedro will be accompanied by Benedick and Claudio, two young nobles. Beatrice seems interested in this news and Leonato mentions a "merry war" between Benedick and Beatrice, suggesting they have a history of banter and sparring.

Messina: a port on the island of Sicily, Italy.

Leonato invites Don Pedro, Benedick, and Claudio to stay with him. Benedick and Beatrice resume their witty back-and-forth, and Claudio develops feelings for Hero, Leonato's daughter. While Benedick loves being a bachelor and scorns marriage, he is unable to persuade Claudio not to marry Hero. Claudio asks Don Pedro to woo her on his behalf at an upcoming Masque ball.

Unfortunately, Don John, Don Pedro's villainous brother, is at the ball and determined to stir up trouble. He tells Claudio that Don Pedro is wooing Hero for himself. However, this misunderstanding is quickly resolved when Claudio confronts the Prince. Claudio and Hero are happily engaged to be married in a week.

Bored at the prospect of waiting a week for the wedding, Don Pedro, Leonato, Hero, and Claudio conspire to set up Benedick and Beatrice by making each one think the other is in love with them. They arrange for both the would-be lovers to overhear conversations about how they are secretly madly in love with each other.

Still determined to embarrass his brother and stop the wedding, Don John plots with Borachio, his servant, to convince Claudio and Don Pedro that Hero is cheating on him. They arrange for Margaret, Hero's maid, to appear at Hero's bedroom window and let Borachio in. Mistaking Margaret for Hero in the dark, Don Pedro and Claudio are taken in by the plot and decide the wedding must be stopped.

The next day at the wedding, Claudio publicly humiliates Hero by calling her false and unfaithful and then storms off as Hero faints. Deeply ashamed, Leonato says he wishes Hero were dead rather than disgraced in this way. However, the Friar officiating the wedding is sympathetic to Hero's plight and tells Leonato and Beatrice they must tell everyone Hero is dead to make Claudio remorseful.

Benedick and Beatrice finally confess their love for each other, but things become tense when she demands that he kill Claudio as revenge for slandering Hero. While Benedick is initially horrified by her request, he trusts Beatrice's judgement of Hero and agrees to challenge his one-time friend to a duel.

Meanwhile, Borachio and his associate, Conrade, have been arrested by the bumbling Watch, led by Constable Dogberry. Despite his idiocy, Dogberry eventually extracts a confession from the pair and reveals the truth about Don John's plot to stop the wedding.

Instead of fighting Claudio, Leonato agrees to forgive him if he marries his niece, who is supposedly almost identical to Hero. Overcome with remorse, Claudio immediately agrees to his request. At the wedding, the bride is revealed to be Hero, still alive, and the pair are happily reunited. Benedick and Beatrice publicly admit their love for each other and agree to be married. They hear news that Don John is returning to the city but a happy Benedick suggests they wait until the following morning to decide his punishment so the couples can enjoy their longed-for marital bliss.

Section 2

Background Information

About the author

William Shakespeare (1564–1516) hardly needs an introduction. Beginning life as the son of a glove-maker in the country town of Stratford-upon-Avon, he rose to popular acclaim in the London theatre scene, writing at least 37 plays and numerous sonnets. He is widely praised as the greatest writer in English and the world's greatest playwright, although his language can often seem obscure to modern day students.

Shakespeare enjoyed great success in London: his plays were popular with rich and poor alike. However, his existence as a playwright was fraught with difficulty: theatres were sometimes closed due to plague outbreaks and the stage was often criticised as scandalous and immoral. Indeed, women were forbidden from acting during Shakespeare's time, so all female characters were played by young boys. Nevertheless, he enjoyed the support of both Queen Elizabeth I and her successor, James I. While many of Shakespeare's ideas can be described as subversive, even proto-feminist, it's not surprising that plays like *Much Ado About Nothing* adhere to a strict social hierarchy. For example, noble characters tend to be more poetic and heroic than their lower-class counterparts.

Subversive: intended to undermine an established system or institution.

About the play

Shakespeare probably wrote *Much Ado About Nothing* in the latter part of 1598, after well-known comedies *The Taming of the Shrew* and *A Midsummer Night's Dream,* but before *As You Like It* and *Twelfth Night.* The only documented performance of the play in Shakespeare's lifetime occurred in 1613 at the marriage of James I's daughter Elizabeth to Prince Frederick of Bohemia. While critics tend to see it as one of Shakespeare's simpler, less morally complex plays, it provides an interesting commentary on marriage, class, and mistaken identity.

Proto-feminist: a term used to describe modern feminist concepts in texts that were written before the advent of feminism.

From the 1530s onwards, there were a series of publications in Elizabethan England that romanticised marriage and provided advice on married life. However, this idyllic view was widely mocked in contemporary literature, theatre, and art, especially through the motifs of cuckoldry and battles of the sexes. *Much Ado About Nothing* reflects both views of marriage: while the ending seems to characterise marriage as merry and blissful, recurring jokes about cuckoldry suggest the characters' deep underlying anxieties about infidelity. Further, Beatrice's feisty spirit suggests a desperate bid for freedom in her last days as an independent, single woman.

Idyllic: perfect, idealised, and blissful.

Cuckoldry: the derision of men ('cuckolds') with unfaithful wives.

Chaste: pure and modest; often this is used to describe virginal women or those who abstain from sex.

Fractious: unruly, difficult to control, or fraught with issues.

Claudio and Hero's love story (sometimes referred to as the main plot), echoes numerous ancient stories about the slandering of **chaste**, innocent women, which have been popular since Biblical times. This type of plot was a recurring trope in contemporary poetry and plays, so we can assume Shakespeare's audience would have been familiar with the narrative. On the other hand, Beatrice and Benedick's story (sometimes called the sub-plot) is more novel: there are no obvious sources for it and it's thought to be Shakespeare's own invention. The differences between the two couples is obvious when we examine how they get to know each other, the language they use to address one another, and the trust (or lack thereof) which exists between them. You can find more information about these differences in the Character Analysis and Key Themes Analysis sections.

It is not surprising that it is Benedick and Beatrice, the 'modern couple,' who have captured more audience and critical interest since the play was first performed. In general, these are the two roles that can make actors famous and many critical essays centre on the unique and **fractious** relationship between the would-be lovers. They have also had a significant impact on popular culture; for instance, King Charles I scribbled "Beatrice and Benedick" over the title of a copy of the play he owned and the French composer Berlioz wrote an opera titled "Beatrice and Benedick" in 1863.

Much Ado About Nothing has been adapted for film multiple times, most recently in 1993 and 2012. If you're looking for a good adaptation, Joss Whedon's 2012 adaptation is a great place to start: Whedon retains most of Shakespeare's script but sets the play in modern times, so it almost feels like a modern day romcom. Even if you haven't read the play yet, it's very accessible and entertaining for 21st century audiences. As with any adaptation, be aware that Whedon made some alterations, such as changing Conrade's gender, and imagining that Benedick and Beatrice have had a sexual relationship before the action of the play starts.

Section 3

Scene-by-Scene Analysis

Act 1 Scene 1

We begin in Messina, Italy. Governor Leonato has just received news (via a messenger) that Don Pedro of Arragon, a prince, is coming to Messina that night to celebrate a recent military campaign. The battle has been a successful one: the Messenger tells Leonato that they have lost "but few of any sort and none of name," indicating that no high-ranking officers have been killed in the combat. This also suggests the value the characters put on social hierarchy: it is the men of rank, and not the foot soldiers, whose lives matter to nobles like Leonato. We also hear that Don Pedro has "bestowed much honour" on Claudio, a young count from Florence, who has proven himself a courageous soldier despite his youth and inexperience.

At this point, Beatrice, Leonato's niece, speaks up to ask if "Signor Mountanto" has returned from the wars. Hero, her cousin, has to explain that she means Benedick, a nobleman from Padua. This nickname for Benedick, which is a fencing term, suggests that he is stuck-up and mocks his apparent skill as a swordsman. The messenger praises Benedick's "good service" in the military, but Beatrice is having none of it: she turns all the messenger's praise of Benedick into clever, witty insults. Leonato intervenes and explains that there is a "merry war" between Benedick and Beatrice, suggesting a history of verbal sparring between the pair.

Don Pedro, Claudio, Benedick, and Balthasar (a servant) arrive, along with Don John, Don Pedro's bastard brother. Leonato is delighted to see the Prince and introduces his daughter, Hero, making a few light-hearted jokes about female infidelity.

Marble-hearted: cold-hearted and devoid of kindness; as though one's heart is made of marble.

Beatrice makes a barbed remark at Benedick, setting off a quick-fire series of witty insults and retorts between the two, during which Beatrice expresses her disgust for male love. Benedick's name for her, "Lady Disdain" recalls the **marble-hearted Petrarchan** beloved (see page 25 for more on Petrarchan love).

Don Pedro interrupts to tell Benedick and Claudio that they have been invited to stay at Leonato's house for at least a month. Leonato personally welcomes Don John, commenting that he has recently been "reconciled" to his brother. All the characters except Benedick and Claudio then depart, leaving the two young men alone on stage.

Petrarchan: a literary term for a lover who is melodramatic and self-consciously suffering.

Claudio confesses that he has fallen in love with Hero. Shocked, Benedick responds cynically and seems perplexed by his friend's sudden infatuation. Claudio, however, is not to be deterred. When Don Pedro returns and learns this news, he seems delighted, commenting that Hero is "very well worthy." This, of course, refers not only to her beauty and disposition but to her noble breeding. Benedick remains cynical, even when his friends call him an "obstinate heretic in the despite of beauty." He responds with a series of jokes about cuckolded husbands, declares that he will never be married, and leaves. Speaking in blank verse, the poetic form reserved for those noble in rank and often when they are speaking in moments of high passion, Claudio tells Don Pedro that before he left for war, he looked on Hero with a "soldier's eye" and could not feel real love for her. However, now that the war is over, he is **besotted.** Don Pedro agrees to woo Hero on Claudio's behalf at the upcoming masque ball that Leonato is hosting in their honour.

Besotted: extremely infatuated.

Act 1 Scene 2

As preparations for the ball get underway, Leonato enters with Antonio, his elderly brother. Antonio tells him that Don Pedro and Claudio have been overheard in the orchard, discussing Claudio's love for Hero and Don Pedro's intention to woo her at the upcoming ball. This foreshadows later scenes in which other conversations are overheard in the orchard. Leonato says that he will "hold it as a dream," not daring to believe the news is true, but that he will tell Hero what he knows so that she will be prepared to answer Don Pedro.

Act 1 Scene 3

Don John enters, with Conrade, his companion. Conrade asks him why he is so melancholy and urges him to "hear reason" and abandon his sadness. Don John, however, is determinedly miserable, saying that he will "claw no man in his humour." This expression means that he won't flatter or fawn over anyone, but also carries a hint of cruelty and sharpness. Conrade advises him not to show his sadness publicly because he is only recently reconciled with his brother and should try and benefit from this newly restored relationship. Don John confesses (for the audience's benefit rather than Conrade's) that he is a "plain-dealing villain" and says that he will not change his behaviour to please his brother, who distrusts him anyway.

Borachio, another companion to Don John, comes in with news of Don Pedro's plans to woo Hero, which he overheard while eavesdropping. Don John seems uplifted by the news and says it may be fuel for some future villainous scheme. Conrade and Borachio affirm their loyalty to him.

Act 2 Scene 1

Meanwhile, Leonato, Antonio, Hero, and Beatrice are waiting for the masque ball to begin. They discuss Don John's sour disposition and Beatrice wittily comments that an ideal man would be midway between Don John, who hardly says anything and Benedick, who talks too much. Leonato and Antonio warn her that she will never get a husband if she continues to be so outspoken but Beatrice replies that she is glad to have no husband. Antonio tells Hero that she should be ruled by her father, and Beatrice mockingly replies that it is Hero's duty to obey him, yet "let him be a handsome fellow, or else make another curtsy and say, father, as it pleases me." This changes the subject of the conversation to female pleasure and implicitly critiques Leonato's domination of his daughter. Leonato tells Beatrice that he hopes to see her "fitted with a husband" one day but she sticks to her line. He also tells Hero that "if the prince do solicit you in that kind, you know your answer."

The dance begins. Pairs of characters move across the stage and we hear snatches of their conversation. First, a disguised Don Pedro invites Hero to dance and they joke about the **grotesque** mask he is wearing. Balthasar, a servant, attempts to flirt with Margaret, one of Hero's gentlewomen. Meanwhile, Ursula, Hero's other gentlewoman, dances with Antonio. He claims not to be Antonio but she sees through his disguise straight away. Finally, we see Benedick and Beatrice. It's not clear whether Beatrice actually doesn't recognise Benedick or if she's merely playing along with the spirit of the masque ball. When Benedick asks her what she thinks of him she replies that "he is the Prince's jester, a very dull fool."

Grotesque: repulsively ugly or distorted in a gruesome, hideous way.

The dance concludes and everyone departs except Don John, Borachio, and Claudio. Pretending to mistake Claudio for Benedick, Don John tells him that he should "**dissuade**" Claudio from marrying Hero because Don John has been wooing her for himself. Claudio is left alone on stage, horrified. He expresses his anguish at Don Pedro's apparent betrayal of him. When Benedick comes to tell him that "the Prince hath got your Hero," Claudio misunderstands him and leaves, angry.

Dissuade: to discourage or disincentivise someone from doing something.

Don Pedro enters and Benedick tells him that Claudio is sulking. Sick of Beatrice's insults, he also rants about Beatrice's performance at the ball, commenting that "she misused me past the endurance of a block." Claudio, Beatrice, Leonato, and Hero come in and Benedick jokingly begs Don Pedro to be excused from Beatrice's company. Don Pedro refuses, but Benedick leaves anyway.

Broker: to arrange or negotiate an agreement between parties.

Don Pedro tells Beatrice that "you have lost the heart of Signor Benedick" and she alludes to a previous, possibly romantic encounter between them. Before we can learn any more about this, however, Leonato and Don Pedro **broker** the match between Claudio and Hero. Claudio, realising his mistake, is joyful, though somewhat subdued. The whole encounter is carried out by **proxy** rather than by the lovers themselves, hinting at Claudio's inadequacy and inexperience.

Proxy: stand-in representatives as substitutes for the real thing.

Struck by Beatrice's vitality, Don Pedro impulsively proposes to her but she declines, suggesting that he is too good for her, and departs. Leonato tells Claudio that he may marry Hero in a week. To keep themselves amused while they wait for the wedding, Leonato, Don Pedro, Claudio, and Hero conspire to bring Benedick and Beatrice into a "mountain of affection" – to set them up as lovers.

Act 2 Scene 2

Frustrated that his scheme has been foiled and that Claudio and Hero are to be married, Don John asks Borachio how he can ruin the wedding. Borachio explains that he has a plan. He is having an ongoing affair with Margaret, Hero's gentlewoman, and can ask her to look out of Hero's bedroom window at any point during the night. Borachio tells Don John to inform Don Pedro and Claudio that Hero is unchaste and disloyal; he should then lead them to where they can see Hero's window. Claudio will mistake Margaret for Hero, become violently jealous, and call off the wedding. Pleased by this plot, Don John goes to find out when Hero and Claudio are to be married.

Act 2 Scene 3

Alone in the orchard, Benedick is frustrated by Claudio's sudden infatuation with Hero. He misses the days when his friend enjoyed the bachelor lifestyle with him and mocked the "shallow follies" of lovers. He wonders if he too, will succumb to a similar infatuation but cannot imagine it, fearing that "love may transform me to an oyster" – a brooding, silent lover who clams up.

Arbor: a garden gazebo or shaded outdoor area.

Seeing Don Pedro, Leonato, Claudio, and Balthasar coming, Benedick hides in the **arbor**. Noticing where Benedick is hiding, the others pretend not to see him and tell Balthasar to sing for them. We then hear *Sigh No More* (see page 35 for more information about this song). From his hiding place, Benedick criticises Balthasar's singing voice, perhaps indicating a general disdain for love songs.

Knowing that Benedick is listening, Don Pedro, Leonato and Claudio begin to discuss Beatrice and her apparent "love" for Benedick. Feigning surprise, Don Pedro remarks that "I thought her spirit had been invincible against all assaults of affection," recalling the recurring metaphor of love as a battleground. While Benedick suspects a trick, he cannot imagine Leonato taking part in such a scheme and becomes more convinced that his friends are telling the truth. They go on to say that Beatrice is nearly dead with lovesickness but that she cannot confess her love; Benedick would surely torment her with it if she did. Eventually they depart, leaving Benedick alone.

Scornfully: expressing contempt or derision.

Flabbergasted, Benedick experiences a sudden change of heart towards love and marriage, declaring that "when I said I would die a bachelor, I did not think I should live til I be married." When Beatrice comes to tell him to come to dinner, he declares "fair Beatrice, I thank you for your pains," to which she responds **scornfully**.

Act 3 Scene 1

Back in the orchard, Hero tells Margaret, her gentlewoman, to fetch Beatrice and tell her to hide in the arbor so she can 'overhear' Margaret and Ursula talking about her. She then directs Ursula that, when Beatrice arrives, they must talk about how lovesick he is for her. In contrast to her subdued **filial** obedience of earlier scenes, Hero seems more **vivacious** here. It's as if she is able to exercise more **agency** among her female companions, as opposed to with men, who don't expect her to have an opinion.

Beatrice hides and Hero and Ursula start talking about Benedick. In contrast to the men's more casual banter in the previous scene, their conversation is in blank verse and rich in metaphor. A series of nature metaphors gives the scene a pleasant, **pastoral** feel, which recalls the coming of spring and the joys of mating and courtship. Knowing that Beatrice is listening, Hero explains that the Prince and Claudio informed her of Benedick's love for Beatrice but that she told them to "wish him wrestle with that affection" (another fighting metaphor for love) because Beatrice is too scornful to ever return his feelings for her.

Shocked at this news and at the way her cousin "condemned" her for being so proud and disdainful, Beatrice vows to change her ways, expressing the desire to "bind our loves up in a holy band."

Act 3 Scene 2

Don Pedro informs Claudio, Benedick, and Leonato that he intends to depart Messina immediately after the wedding. Ever loyal to the Prince and eager to please, Claudio offers to go with him to Arragon but Don Pedro urges him to stay and enjoy his honeymoon, he will take Benedick with him instead. Initially, this interaction seems jarring: why would Don Pedro go to such lengths to bring Benedick and Beatrice together if he is planning to take Benedick away so soon? The simplest explanation is that he doesn't take anything very seriously: his matchmaking is mere sport before the wedding festivities and he doesn't expect to see it followed through.

Benedick's friends notice his changed demeanour and ask him what's happened, but he claims to have a toothache. Claudio and Don Pedro remain convinced that he is in love – they even notice that he has shaved off his beard (Beatrice earlier remarked that she couldn't abide men with beards). Benedick and Leonato depart and the others think that Benedick may be asking his permission to court Beatrice.

Suddenly, Don John comes in to inform Claudio of Hero's disloyalty. While Claudio and Don Pedro are both shocked and disbelieving, they agree to accompany him that night to see if Hero comes out to talk to anyone at the window.

Filial: the sense of duty and loyalty from a child to their parents.

Vivacious: lively, animated, and in high-spirits.

Agency: the capacity to act freely and make one's own choices.

Pastoral: like a peaceful country landscape; often an idealised image of rural life.

Act 3 Scene 3

Malapropism: using an incorrect word instead of the correct, similar sounding word.

In an abrupt change of pace, we are introduced to Dogberry, the Chief Constable of the Watch and Verges, his sidekick, along with other members of the watch – Messina's police force. Dogberry is a bumbling, comic figure who constantly uses **malapropisms**. A man named George Seacoal is selected to be constable and to supervise the watch on Dogberry's behalf. Dogberry tries to inform the Watch of the best ways to protect Messina but ends up setting out a plan of inaction: he advises them not to arrest a hypothetical thief but to "let him show himself what he is and let him steal out of your company." Bidding the Watch goodnight, Dogberry reminds them of the upcoming wedding and advises them to keep an eye on things at Leonato's house.

Dogberry and Verges leave and Conrade comes in with an obviously drunk Borachio. Gleefully, Borachio confesses Don John's entire plot and how he has been paid handsomely for his part in it. He also tells Conrade that Claudio expressed his intention to "before the whole congregation shame [Hero]."

Unfortunately for Conrade and Borachio, Seacoal and other members of the watch have overheard the whole exchange and they are arrested immediately.

Act 3 Scene 4

Bawdily: in a way that is humorous and sexually suggestive.

On the morning of the wedding, Margaret and Ursula are helping Hero choose a dress and complimenting her appearance. When Hero confesses to being heavy-hearted (perhaps a sense of foreboding), Margaret **bawdily** remarks that "'Twill be heavier soon with the weight of a husband", a joke which is typical of her outspoken nature.

Beatrice enters and the others notice her changed demeanour. Not wanting to admit her feelings for Benedick, she claims to be sick. Margaret continues to provoke her by talking about Benedick until Ursula announces that the men have arrived to take Hero to the church to be married.

Act 3 Scene 5

Arrant: an old English word meaning complete or absolute.

Knave: a dishonest, unscrupulous man.

Dogberry and Verges inform Leonato that they have now arrested "a couple of as **arrant knaves** as any in Messina" and ask if he can question them. Unfortunately, Leonato is in a hurry to get to the wedding and, frustrated by their bumbling explanations, he sends them away to question the villains themselves. They agree to this and head to the gaol so they can record the interview.

Act 4 Scene 1

All the noble characters gather in church for Claudio and Hero's wedding. When the Friar asks if Claudio has come to church to marry Hero, he boldly replies "no." Leonato, missing the threat, assumes that Claudio is playing on the double grammar of *marry* and playfully replies "to be married *to* her."

To Hero, Beatrice, and Leonato's shock, Claudio abruptly begins to denounce Hero as an unchaste "rotten orange." Leonato tries to console him, saying that if he slept with Hero before the wedding, they may still be married. Claudio, however, continues to rail against Hero's "seeming" and way she appears so chaste and virginal despite her apparent "sin."

His use of elaborate figures of speech and **oxymorons** of fair foulness strengthen the emotional quality of the scene. While Hero tries to deny his accusations, her protests are interrupted by Claudio, and both Don Pedro and Don John step forward to confirm his story. Don John seems particularly **malicious** here, as he mockingly tells Hero "pretty lady / I am sorry much for thy misgovernment" (note the informal use of *thy* to address a social inferior).

Oxymoron: a contradiction in terms (e.g. tiny giant, loud silence).

At this point, Hero falls into a death-like faint from shock. Leonato remarks that death is, perhaps, the best outcome for Hero now that her reputation lies in ruins. He laments the way he cherished Hero in the past and the shame that will fall upon his noble house because of her actions. Benedick urges Leonato to be patient and let matters come to light and asks Beatrice if she shared Hero's bed last night. Alas, she did not, so can provide no alibi for her innocent cousin.

Malicious: having evil or cruel intent to harm another person.

The Friar, who was officiating the wedding, speaks up and says that he believes Hero is the victim of some "biting error" – he observed her reacting in disbelief and horror to the slander and believes her to be genuine. While Leonato is doubtful at first, he eventually agrees to listen to the Friar's plan – especially when Benedick points out that Don John could be behind the accusations. The Friar tells Leonato that he must pretend that Hero is dead so that Claudio, overcome with guilt and remorse, will regret the slander and mourn her beauty. He tries to console Hero, suggesting that "This wedding day / Perhaps is but prolonged."

Friar Francis, Leonato, and Hero depart, leaving Benedick and Beatrice alone on stage. Prompted by the stress of the occasion, they confess their love for each other, but Beatrice is out for revenge. When Benedick asks what he can do for her, she asks him to "Kill Claudio." She grieves the fact that, as a woman, she cannot challenge Claudio to a duel and avenge Hero's shame. When Benedick refuses, she lashes out at him, accusing men of being good for words and nothing else. Reluctantly, he agrees to challenge Claudio.

Act 4 Scene 2

Meanwhile, Dogberry and Verges are questioning Conrade and Borachio in front of a **sexton**. The whole process is muddled because of Dogberry's idiotic confusion but he eventually calls forth Seacoal to tell the sexton what he witnessed last night. We learn that Don John has fled Messina, thus incriminating him and his accomplices. Frustrated, Conrade calls Dogberry an ass, which Dogberry is mortally offended by.

Sexton: a caretaker of a church and its graveyard.

Act 5 Scene 1

Some time later, Leonato is talking to Antonio about his grief over Hero's slander. In contrast to earlier scenes, he seems more sad than angry and resists Antonio's attempts to comfort him. Having reflected on the matter, he is also more inclined to believe Hero's version of events.

Don Pedro and Claudio come in, causing Leonato and Antonio to become furious. Leonato informs them that their slander has killed the innocent Hero and Antonio delivers biting insults, accusing the two men of being "boys, apes, braggarts, Jacks, milksops". Exasperated, Don Pedro defends Claudio, saying that Hero was accused of nothing except "what was true, and very full of proof.".Leonato and Antonio depart.

Benedick enters, ready to challenge Claudio to a duel. At first, Don Pedro and Claudio joke with him, assuming his threats are merely idle banter. Even when they realise he isn't jesting, Claudio refuses to take the challenge seriously, instead choosing to mock Benedick's newfound affection for Beatrice. Undeterred, Benedick dismisses his friends' attitudes as "gossip-like humour," hinting at their immaturity. He also tells them that Don John has fled Messina, immediately arousing Don Pedro's suspicions, but promptly departs before they can ask him more.

Dogberry and Verges bring in Conrade and Borachio to inform Leonato of their crimes. Dogberry, as usual, is bumbling and confusing, but Borachio steps in and confesses the whole evil scheme. Shocked and overcome with guilt, Claudio realises his mistake.

Epitaph: an inscription on a grave to commemorate someone's memory.

Leonato returns and Claudio begs him to punish him in any way he wishes. Leonato declines this offer, instead asking Claudio and Don Pedro to write an **epitaph** for Hero's tomb and "sing it to her bones" that night. Tomorrow morning, he tells them, Claudio may be married to Antonio's daughter, who is supposedly nearly identical to Hero. Claudio is relieved and overjoyed at Leonato's sudden change of heart and agrees to this plan immediately.

Leonato plans to question Margaret, who he believes was part of the plot to defame Hero. Borachio, however, defends her, saying she acted innocently and had no idea what she was doing.

Act 5 Scene 2

Immediately after challenging Claudio, Benedick asks Margaret to tell him where Beatrice is. Sassy as ever, Margaret exchanges a few witty retorts with him but eventually goes to call Beatrice.

Alone, Benedick laments that he was "not born under a rhyming planet" so he cannot write a sonnet for Beatrice. The rhymes he attempts – "lady/baby," "school/fool," "scorn/horn" – once again address his **latent** fear of cuckoldry and being forced to father his wife's illegitimate child, thereby becoming her fool.

Beatrice arrives, but refuses to kiss him until he reveals that he has challenged Claudio to a duel. Soon after, Ursula enters to inform them that the plot against Hero has been exposed and urges them to come to Leonato.

Latent: something that is hidden or concealed, and has not yet manifested and come to light; a dormant trait or emotion that is yet to come to the surface.

Act 5 Scene 3

At Hero's tomb that night, Don Pedro and Claudio present the epitaph and song they have written in memory of her. You can find a more detailed analysis of the song on page 35. As the sun rises, Don Pedro tells Claudio it is time to go to Leonato's and meet his new bride.

Act 5 Scene 4

Leonato, Friar Francis, Benedick, Antonio, Margaret, Ursula, and Hero enter. All seem glad that Hero's innocence has finally been proved and that Benedick is no longer obliged to fight Claudio. Leonato tells Hero and the other women to withdraw and return, masked, when Claudio arrives. Benedick asks Leonato for Beatrice's hand in marriage, which he gladly gives.

Don Pedro and Claudio arrive, ready for the wedding. They mock Benedick's newfound desire to be married but this time he plays along, happy to be on good terms again.

Leonato presents Hero to Claudio as his new bride but refuses to let him see her face until he takes her hand in front of the Friar and agrees to marry her. When he realises his new wife is none other than Hero, Claudio is astonished and **jubilant.**

Jubilant: feeling profound happiness or triumph.

Meanwhile, Benedick asks which one of the masked women is Beatrice. Despite their earlier declarations of love, they seem hesitant to declare it in front of the crowd: when asked if she loves Benedick, Beatrice coyly replies "no more than reason." Claudio and Hero, however, know better, producing sonnets written by the couple to each other that they never delivered. While Beatrice protests that "I yield upon great persuasion," Benedick kisses her, silencing her sparkling wit.

Don Pedro and Claudio continue to mock Benedick's change of heart, but he replies that "man is a giddy thing" and defends his sudden choice to marry with good humour. He remarks that Don Pedro is sad and tells him to "get thee a wife."

A messenger enters and tells Don Pedro that Don John has been arrested. Benedick tells him that this can wait until morning – for now is the time to dance and be merry.

Section 4

Character Analysis

Beatrice

Beatrice is the niece of Leonato, governor of Messina. Feisty and sharp-tongued, she subverts the Elizabethan expectation of the modest, dutiful maiden embodied by her cousin Hero, to whom she is fiercely devoted, and is frustrated by the lack of agency afforded to women in her culture. Her name means *one who blesses,* implicitly linking her to Benedick, whose name means *blessed.*

While some sources list Beatrice as Antonio's daughter, there is more textual evidence to support her being an orphan: she is far more independent than the filial Hero and does not defer to Antonio's authority at any point. Further, Antonio makes no attempt to control her or to **cajole** her into getting married when she initially refuses to take a husband. Indeed, no one seems very concerned by Beatrice's refusal to marry – the other characters only conspire to bring her together with Benedick as a form of amusement.

Cajole: attempting to persuade someone to do something by coaxing or enticing them.

Beatrice is free-spirited and unafraid to enter the world of male conversation. For example, in Act 2 Scene 1, she tells Claudio "speak, count, 'tis your cue" and playfully teases him about being "something of that jealous complexion" in front of Don Pedro. She exhibits none of the modesty expected of a maiden eligible to be married. Far from detracting from her beauty, her disdainful humour **beguiles** both the audience and the other characters. In Act 2 Scene 1, there is an awkward moment in which Don Pedro asks "will you have me, lady?" – so attracted by her vivacious wit that he impulsively proposes to her. Beatrice wisely replies that "your grace is too costly to wear every day," knowing that, as a commoner and an orphan, she would be an unsuitable wife for a prince.

Beguile: to fool or deceive via misleading appearances.

As the more assertive, confident cousin, most critics believe Beatrice to be older than Hero. While Shakespeare does not explicitly state his characters' ages, the suggestion of a past relationship between Benedick and Beatrice supports this view – see Act 2 Scene 1:

> QUOTES :
>
> **Don Pedro:** Come, lady, come, you have lost the heart of Signor Benedick.
>
> **Beatrice:** Indeed, my lord, he lent it me a while, and I gave him use for it, a double heart for his single one, marry once before he won it of me with false dice, therefore your grace may well say I have lost it.

Here, Beatrice is playing on the idea of lovers exchanging hearts: she gave him hers but Benedick only "lent" his and took it back, meaning he possessed a "double heart."

While this was no doubt a sad occasion for Beatrice, the wordplay makes light of her sorrow as she affects an air of proud **apathy** towards Benedick.

Apathy: lack of emotion, interest, or enthusiasm.

From the beginning of the play, the similarities between Benedick and Beatrice are striking – not least in terms of their scorn for marriage. In Act 1 Scene 1, Beatrice comments that "I had rather hear my dog bark at a crow than hear a man say he loved me" and Benedick expresses similar sentiments in response to Claudio's gushing infatuation with Hero. In many ways, the pair are more reminiscent of Shakespearean clowns than lovers.

However, after the aborted wedding scene, the play takes on a distinctly darker tone and underlying gender tensions are brought to light. Appalled at the slander of her innocent cousin, Beatrice declares "oh God that I were a man! I would eat [Claudio's] heart in the marketplace," expressing her anguish at her powerlessness to avenge Hero. The mention of the marketplace, an explicitly public space, suggests Beatrice's exclusion from the male-coded world of honour and vengeance. By coercing Benedick to challenge Claudio to a duel, Beatrice makes him her instrument of revenge, forcing him to stand against the misogyny which undoes her cousin.

Before this promise can be fulfilled, however, Hero's honour is restored and the play ends on the happy prospect of a double wedding. Unlike Hero, who is once again 'given' to Claudio by her father, Beatrice unveils herself out of choice to ask Benedick "What is thy will?" (This is also a cheeky **double entendre** – the word *will* had sexual connotations which would have been obvious to Shakespeare's audience). While the pair may joke that they only love each other out of pity, the audience knows better – this is, we hope, a true marriage of minds which will result in lasting happiness.

Double entendre: a phrase with two interpretations, one of which is sexual or otherwise indecent and risqué.

Benedick

Benedick is a successful soldier and close companion of Don Pedro and Claudio. Unlike Claudio, he lacks respect for the Prince's noble authority and adopts a cynical, somewhat mocking demeanour toward the outside world – although there is an undercurrent of vulnerability beneath this bravado. He shares Beatrice's scornful view of marriage and seems exasperated with Claudio's sudden decision to marry Hero. However, the aborted wedding causes him to reconsider his relationship to Beatrice, and his place within the **chauvinist** masculine world in which her cousin was unfairly slandered.

Chauvinist: a person displaying aggressive dominance or arrogance, typically at over or at the expense of women.

From the beginning of the play, it is clear that Benedick and Claudio share a brotherly relationship: he is the first person Claudio confides in when he finds himself smitten with Hero. In contrast to Claudio, who is afraid to trust his own judgement, Benedick speaks with the natural arrogance of one who thinks he understands everything. In response to Claudio's outpouring of superficial desire, he drily replies "I can see yet without spectacles and I see no such matter," grounding his perception of Hero in the real, seen world as opposed to Claudio's Petrarchan fantasy.

However, Shakespeare suggests that both are distorted ways of seeing: while Claudio may be naïve and gullible, Benedick represses his obvious attraction to Beatrice as he clings to the sexual and personal freedom afforded to him as a young bachelor.

Partly, this disdain for marriage is motivated by the same cuckoldry anxiety that proves Claudio's undoing – Benedick's lines in this scene are peppered with references to horns, a traditional symbol of cuckoldry (see page 34). Like the archetypal Elizabethan fool (Beatrice calls him "the prince's jester"), Benedick inhabits a space outside social convention: his clowning behaviour is markedly less serious than his fellow courtesans and he is reluctant to follow societal norms by submitting to a 'good' marriage. Consider his monologue in Act 2 Scene 3, where he expresses his frustration with Claudio's sudden infatuation. Where once Benedick and Claudio laughed at the "shallow follies" of men who fall in love, Claudio has now become, in Benedick's eyes, "the argument of his own scorn," the butt of the jokes he once made. Further, Benedick fears that "love may transform me to an oyster," creating the idea of a brooding lover who clams up, oyster-like, no longer full of wit and **mirth**.

Mirth: amusement or merriment.

Of course, the main purpose of this speech is to set up the dramatic irony of the following exchange, where Benedick is so struck by Don Pedro's (false) revelation that Beatrice loves him that he declares "I will be horribly in love with her." Part of what attracts him to Beatrice is her similar scorn for social convention. Consider this exchange from Act 2 Scene 1:

> QUOTES :
>
> **Beatrice:** We must follow the leaders.
>
> **Benedick:** In every good thing.
>
> **Beatrice:** Nay, if they lead to any ill, I will leave them at the next turning.

In this context, Beatrice is suggesting they must move on in the courtly dance in which they are taking part. However, the second, underlying meaning is that Beatrice will only follow social convention so far – she would not, for example, follow the Prince's noble authority if it led to moral wrongdoing ("any ill").

This seemingly innocuous exchange becomes relevant in Act 4, where Don Pedro and Claudio falsely accuse Hero of infidelity. When Benedick tells Beatrice "surely I do believe your fair cousin is wronged," he becomes the only male character to believe Hero. He opposes Leonato, Don Pedro (his former commanding officer), and the misogynist **mores** which dictate Hero must be guilty until proven innocent. It is unsurprising, then, that in response to Beatrice's demand that he kill Claudio, he initially declares "Ha! Not for the wide world."

Mores: societal standards, customs, or conventions.

However, Benedick has been transformed by love and reluctantly realises that, as actions speak louder than words, he must challenge Claudio to a duel: he declares "enough, I am engaged, I will challenge him." Where before Benedick was the "prince's jester," he now **spurns** the Prince and Claudio's "gossip-like humour" and bears his challenge straight and to the point.

Spurn: to reject with disdain or contempt.

Since this is a comedy, the fateful duel never materialises, and the fractious conflict is replaced by the joy of a double wedding. Paradoxically, Benedick takes on the assertive role of the husband which he earlier seemed to criticise, stopping Beatrice's mouth with a kiss and ordering the musicians to "strike up."

Hero

Hero is the daughter of Leonato, governor of Messina, and cousin to Beatrice. She is betrothed to Claudio until he ruins their wedding by denouncing her as unfaithful. Somewhat timid, Hero often seems to lack agency and her reputation proves more important to the plot than her feelings or beliefs. However, she shows great resourcefulness when **gulling** Beatrice into a romance with Benedick and it would be wrong to characterise her as a mere non-entity.

Gulling: fooling or deceiving someone.

Although she is heir to Leonato's estates, Hero seems to live in the shadow of her more vivacious cousin. In the opening scene, her only line of dialogue is to clarify something Beatrice said to the messenger. It is clear that the two cousins care deeply for one another: Hero later tells Don Pedro that "I will do any modest office... to help my cousin to a good husband." She is Leonato's sole heir, and often seems dominated by his wishes. For example, in the betrothal scene (Act 2 Scene 1), Leonato declares "Count, take of me my daughter, and with her my fortunes" – a timely reminder that this marriage is not only a love match but also a financial exchange between two noble families. Hero says nothing, her consent to the marriage not being needed or asked for. It is Beatrice who prompts her out of passivity, saying "speak, cousin, or (if you cannot) stop his mouth with a kiss, so he may not speak neither," subtly undermining Claudio's masculine authority.

While it's easy to describe Hero as passive and meek in comparison to Beatrice's **brazen** sass, her role in bringing Benedick and Beatrice together is not to be overlooked. In Act 3 Scene 1, her opening monologue (and the first time we have heard her speak at length) is full of **imperatives** to Margaret – "run thee to the parlour," "whisper her ear," and "leave us alone." This indicates that Hero is using the soft power available to her as a woman to her advantage, determined not to be left out of the men's amusing schemes. Further, it shows that Hero is not voiceless but rather accustomed to being spoken for, or about, by men. In this scene, we can also observe her excitement about her upcoming wedding; when Ursula asks when she is to be married, she replies "why every day tomorrow." In modern English, this means 'from tomorrow, I shall be a married woman every day!' indicating her high spirits and optimism about the future as she rushes to choose a dress for the occasion. While Beatrice rails against the lack of liberties afforded to her sex, Hero finds joy in traditional femininity.

Brazen: bold and shameless.

Imperative: a grammatical term for commands or instructional phrases.

As events escalate and Don John's villainous scheme comes to fruition, Hero's blackened name becomes more central to the scandal than Hero herself. See this exchange in Act 4 Scene 1:

Catechising: a term from Catholicism used to describe an interrogation in the form of questions and answers.

> QUOTES :
> **Hero:** Oh God defend me, how I am beset!
> What kind of **catechising** call you this?
> **Claudio:** To make you answer truly to your name.
> **Hero:** Is it not Hero? Who can blot that name
> With any just reproach?

Aghast: filled with horror or shock.

Mutable: prone to changing or transforming.

Note Hero's references to God and *catechism* – a formal question and answer summary of Christian religious principles. This shows Hero desperately trying to assert her purity before God as her honour comes under attack. Claudio replies in the same vein – the first question in the Church of England catechism is 'What is your name?' Beyond religious ideals, Hero is **aghast** that, as an obedient noblewoman, she should be attacked and slandered in this way; her identity as Hero, Leonato's daughter, along with her innocence, should be enough to save her from shame and "any just reproach." However, within the play's atmosphere of disguise and illusion, the notion of innocence is **mutable**, manipulated by Don John's scheme and Claudio's gullible noting. Hero's subsequent counterfeit death, then, is not merely a trick to win back Claudio but also a representation of how shame impacts her: for someone who, up until this point, has been valued solely for her status as an eligible young heiress, slander *is* death.

Claudio

Claudio is a young gallant, companion to Don Pedro and friend to Benedick. He is an accomplished soldier who is praised for "doing in the figure of a lamb the feats of a lion." However, he is more naïve in the affairs of love. Initially smitten with Hero, his feelings towards her abruptly change when he falls for Don John's villainous scheme and sabotages his own wedding as a result.

Laud: to give high praise; extol or celebrate.

Claudio enjoys a brotherly bond with both Don Pedro and Benedick, a relationship which has no doubt been strengthened by their time on the battlefield together. For example, in Act 1 Scene 2, Claudio asks for Benedick's "sober judgement" on whether Hero would make a suitable match for him, demonstrating his regard for his friend's advice. Benedick's response is typical: he comments that "methinks she's too low for a high praise, too brown for a fair praise and too little for a great praise," indulging in the kind of comradely mockery that makes Beatrice call him "the prince's jester." Claudio, however, is more solemn: in awe, he asks "can the world buy such a jewel?" This echoes the Petrarchan tradition of **lauding** a woman's physical attributes using simile, and also reminds the audience that, as an heiress, Hero is a worthy financial match for the young count. In comparison to Benedick and Beatrice, Claudio and Hero's marriage is not so much a love-match as an arranged union of two young, wealthy people, which is perhaps why he is so vulnerable to fears of cuckoldry.

From the beginning of the play, Claudio's deep-seated cuckoldry anxiety renders him rather suggestible to rumour and gossip. As a strict adherent to social hierarchy, Claudio naturally believes that the prince, his social superior, will be better placed to woo Hero than himself, so asks him to approach her at the masque ball. However, this strategy proves flawed when he is told by Don John that the Prince wants Hero for himself. Here, Claudio consoles himself with a set of self pitying generalisations – "beauty is a witch / Against whose charms faith melteth into blood." Like the archetypal cuckold, he seems oddly passive: he neither plots revenge nor takes steps to see if the rumours are true. This lack of agency is also present in the betrothal scene, where Hero is passed like a silent commodity from her father to the Prince, and only then to Claudio. While silent obedience on Hero's part is to be expected of a woman, Claudio's silence is perplexing. A nobleman about to be married should be assertively celebrating the occasion, not having to be prompted by Beatrice – "speak, count, 'tis your cue."

Apart from being timid and inadequate, Claudio's **hamartia** is his failure to see beyond outward appearances. When he denounces Hero as unfaithful, he rails against her apparently deceptive looks – "she's but the sign and **semblance** of her honour." Ironically, he fails to see that his 'reality' is also mere "seeming," a story constructed by Don John to ruin the wedding. Perhaps it is cuckoldry anxiety which makes him more inclined to assume Margaret must be Hero: deep down, he assumes he will inevitably be abandoned for a worthier sexual partner.

Hamartia: a fatal flaw leading to a character's tragic downfall.

Semblance: outward appearance or form.

Even after Hero's good name is restored and he agrees once again to marry her, his language is concerned with surface level appearances:

> QUOTES :
> **Claudio:** "Good Hero, now thy image doth appear
> In the rare semblance that I loved it first."

Unlike Benedick and Beatrice, Claudio has failed to progress from his initial worldview. Even his closing communication with Hero is brief and stilted, suggesting the continuation of his inadequacy into the apparently blissful world of marriage.

Don Pedro

Don Pedro is a visiting Prince from Aragon, former commanding officer of Claudio and Benedick and friend to Leonato. While his noble authority carries much weight in Messina, there is a certain carefree youthfulness about him to suggest he is younger than Leonato, perhaps not much older than Claudio and Benedick, with whom he shares a deep friendship.

Benevolent: kind-hearted, or well-intentioned.

Curt: rudely brief, terse, and abrupt.

Misogyny: prejudice against women, or the belief that men are superior.

Dichotomy: a division between two completely opposing traits or concepts.

Cupid: the Roman god of desire and attraction, often portrayed as a cherub or angel with a bow and arrow he shoots at lovers.

In Messina's landscape of mistaken identity and manipulation, Don Pedro is broadly a **benevolent** presence, although his mistake nearly costs Hero her life. Prior to the beginning of the play, we presume he has righteously triumphed over his brother and tried to effect a reconciliation by welcoming him to Messina with open arms, rather than imprisoning him. While Don John's villainy may seem obvious to an audience – his **curt** silences, his scheming, the way he's often dressed entirely in black by directors – Don Pedro is a generously inclined character who wants to share his good fortune with others. Even his false condemnation of Hero as a "common stale" stems from a righteous desire to protect Claudio, his friend, from shame and scandal. This is, of course, casually **misogynistic** but it is a misogyny shaped by cultural mores as well as an all-pervading sense of cuckoldry anxiety, rather than malicious hatred of women.

Interestingly, Don Pedro stands out as a single nobleman among the happy scenes of wooing which play out in Messina. Symmetrically, this links him to his brother, John the bastard: they are both single men flanked by two young gallants. Don Pedro is the light which contrasts with Don John's darkness, the matchmaker to Don John's matchbreaker, encapsulating the classic good vs. evil **dichotomy** which is typical of a comedy. In both plot and sub-plot (if Benedick and Beatrice can rightly be called a sub-plot), Don Pedro is the architect of romance, wooing Hero on behalf of Claudio and promising to bring Benedick and Beatrice into a "mountain of affection" through an elaborate scheme of overheard gossip. Meanwhile, John schemes to undo his brother's good work through a series of malicious hoaxes. Don Pedro's role in the play is rather like the mythical **cupid**: he even jokes that "if we can [bring Benedick and Beatrice together], Cupid is no longer an archer, his glory shall be ours, for we are the only love-gods."

However, for all his apparent skill as a matchmaker, Don Pedro is no match for Benedick in either wit or social power. After he witnesses what he thinks is Hero being unfaithful, the Prince is transformed from confident "love-god" to Don John's fool. Even here, he remains loyal to Claudio – he vows that "as I wooed for thee to obtain her, I will join with thee to disgrace her." At the aborted wedding, it is Benedick, and not Don Pedro, who suspects Don John of renewed treachery, suggesting that, like Claudio, Don Pedro struggles to see beyond the surface of events.

Since this is a comedy, Don Pedro takes no blame for his part in the slander: he has been duped and the other characters immediately accept this. It's worth noting, however, his lack of agency at the end of the play. While the messenger's words "my lord, your brother John is ta'en in flight" are addressed to Don Pedro, it is Benedick who answers him, indicating a shift in the social order. Having been a dupe, the legitimacy of Don Pedro's authority is reduced – all that he retains is his title and class privilege.

Leonato

Leonato is the governor of Messina, Hero's father, and Beatrice's uncle. A benevolent **patriarch**, he willingly extends his hospitality to Don Pedro and his entire entourage. While some editions of the play list a non-speaking wife in the *dramatis personae*, he appears as single, probably widowed, in most productions.

At the beginning of the play, it is clear that Leonato takes pleasure in surrounding himself with people: he tells Don Pedro that "when you depart from me, happiness takes his leave and sadness abides." He delights in playing the perfect host – even to the villains of the piece. In contrast to Benedick and Beatrice, he represents the conventional noble establishment: he gives his daughter away like a commodity to a man she barely knows and scolds Beatrice that "thou wilt never get thee a husband, if thou be so shrewd of thy tongue." While he never expresses any unkindness towards his niece, it's clear that her feisty spirit and independence sets him on edge.

The true tragedy of Leonato's character is his obsession with reputation: after Hero is slandered and faints, he remarks that "death is the fairest cover for her shame." Even to an Elizabethan audience, this is shocking: Leonato is saying he would rather Hero were dead than her reputation be damaged. He rails against his daughter, barely giving her time to draw breath and deny the accusations. Of course, this is partly motivated by the devastation of his social and financial legacy: Hero is his sole heir, and if she is no longer eligible to be married, that would mean the end of his noble dynasty. Further, his idealised image of his daughter as a virginal, pure woman has been destroyed. The Prince and Claudio, he feels, cannot be lying – his respect for Don Pedro's noble authority **precludes** this; therefore Hero must be tainted.

After his violent outburst at the aborted wedding, Leonato becomes more contemplative and sad, perhaps under the influence of the clever friar. He confides in his brother that "my soul doth tell me, Hero is **belied**,", becoming more open to the possibility of a mistake and enraged at Claudio. Generosity, however, or perhaps respect for social convention, prevents him from exacting revenge: he accepts that Claudio was duped and gives away Hero once again. For Leonato, the **auspicious** marriage proves more important than the events that preceded it and he delights in celebrating the happy occasion with his reputation intact.

Patriarch: the male head of a household.

Dramatis personae: a list of characters in a play at the start of a text.

Preclude: to prevent something from happening, or to make something impossible.

Belied: to be portrayed in a way that gives a false or contradictory impression of a person or idea.

Auspicious: favourable, or conducive to success; a positive sign of prosperity and good things to come.

Don John

Don John is Don Pedro's bastard (illegitimate) brother and the villain of the play. From opening act, there is a certain malevolence to John – he is often dressed entirely in funereal black and admits that "I am not of many words," creating the impression of sullen brooding in contrast to the other nobles' **loquacious** banter.

Unlike the villains in Shakespeare's tragedies, Don John has no complex motive apart from envy for his brother's social authority. As a bastard, he has no inheritance or power, meaning he must rely on his cunning to make his way in the world. He seems to have a history of treachery: Conrade tells him that "you have lately stood out against your brother, and he hath ta'en you newly into his grace." Don John's jealousy, however, remains: he remarks that "it better fits my blood to be **disdained** of all, than to fashion a carriage to rob love from any." Here, we see his natural **misanthropy**: he sees love as something stolen, rather than earned or given freely.

In a play full of contented, benevolent characters, Don John is a walking darkness, the matchbreaker to his brother's matchmaker. In the scenes leading up to Hero's slander, he is carefully **ambiguous**: he teases Don Pedro and Claudio, his victims, with half-truths and innuendo, playing on their latent fears of cuckoldry. By creating the scene at the window, he sets up an impossible choice between spoiled love and intact honour, rushing Claudio into trusting the 'evidence' of his eyes above any rational judgement. At the height of his **pyrrhic victory**, he taunts Hero, calling her "pretty lady" and mocking her "misgovernment."

Don John's absence from the end of the play is somewhat ambiguous. It could be an auspicious sign: the villains are arrested and absent so the central characters can join hands in a merry dance and enjoy a fairytale ending. Nevertheless, his darkness remains, lurking as yet unpunished outside this merry circle, a sinister reminder that love can be manipulated and betrayed.

Margaret

Margaret is a gentlewoman attending Beatrice and Hero. While she lacks the class privilege afforded to the two noblewomen, she is intelligent and quick-witted and loves to shock with audacious bawdy jokes. Margaret's pivotal role in the plot happens offstage, when she appears at Hero's window to meet Borachio as part of the ruse devised by Don John. This appears to be part of an ongoing love affair – Borachio confesses that "I can at any unseasonable instant of the night, appoint her to look out her lady's chamber window." While the consequences of her actions are disastrous, Margaret faces little retribution and seems more a pawn than a willing accomplice – at least according to Borachio. While Shakespeare leaves open the possibility that Borachio is merely protecting his lover, it's easy to imagine Margaret staying silent after Hero's denunciation for fear of punishment by Leonato. In a society obsessed with virginity, her behaviour is outrageous even for a lower-class character – so it's also possible she stays silent for fear of scandal.

Loquacious: talkative.

Disdained: expressing disinterest, as though things are unworthy of one's consideration.

Misanthropy: hatred or contempt for all of humanity.

Ambiguous: open to multiple interpretations, or having more than one meaning.

Pyrrhic victory: a success that comes at too great a cost to have been worthwhile to the victor; an empty or hollow victory.

Ursula

Ursula is the other waiting gentlewoman attending Hero. Unlike Margaret, she is more uptight and less inclined to tease and joke with her social superiors. Her major role in the plot is to assist Hero to convince Beatrice that Benedick is hopelessly in love with her.

Borachio

Borachio is one of Don John's followers and the architect of the nearly fatal plot to smear Hero's honour. His name comes from the Spanish *borracho* – drunk – and it is his drunken confession to Conrade which proves his undoing. Although he is Don John's social inferior, Borachio is perhaps more intelligent: after all, it is his evil genius which conceives the illusion of Margaret at the window. Nevertheless, Borachio is not without remorse. In response to Leonato's accusation that Margaret was "packed in all this wrong," Borachio passionately defends her innocence: he claims that she "always hath been just and virtuous / In anything that I do know by her." Unlike Don John, Borachio bears no real malice towards the Prince or Hero, he is merely a **mercenary** who is happy to accept money from unsavoury people.

Mercenary: a professional soldier who works for a salary.

Conrade

Conrade is another of Don John's followers. While he plays no instrumental role in the villainous plot, he seems entirely devoted to Don John and admiring of his villainy. Some modern productions portray Conrade as Don John's lover.

Dogberry

Dogberry is the Chief Constable of the Watch, or the Chief of Police, in Messina. Much like the archetypal Elizabethan fool, Dogberry's main role is to provide comic relief. Here, however, the comic relief is unintentional. Compared to Benedick and Beatrice's clever punning, Dogberry simply does not know what the correct word to use is, resulting in many malapropisms. This can also be viewed as a class satire – Dogberry is an earnest, middle class man trying to make an honest living and thinks that, by using flowery language, he can become like the nobles.

Verges

Verges is Dogberry's equally idiotic deputy. He shares Dogberry's habit of using many malapropisms.

Antonio

Antonio is Leonato's brother and Hero's uncle. He is described as an "old man," so perhaps a little older than the middle-aged Leonato, who still seems full of life. He seems to share many of his brother's conservative views towards marriage and women – he tells Hero "I trust you will be ruled by your father," while they wait for the masque ball to begin. After the aborted wedding scene, Antonio acts as Leonato's close friend and confidante in his grief, counselling him that "if you go on thus, you will kill yourself."

Interestingly, the typically peaceable Antonio is less forgiving of Claudio and Don Pedro than his brother – he calls them "scambling, out-facing, fashion-monging boys," suggesting that their youth has led them to make poor choices. While Leonato seems shocked by his brother's outburst, nothing comes of it. As an elderly man, Antonio cannot challenge either young man to a duel and must wait for the Friar's plan to come to fruition.

Friar Francis

Friar Francis officiates Claudio and Hero's wedding ceremony. Apart from Benedick, he is the only male character to believe in Hero's innocence, remarking that "and in her eye there hath appeared a fire / To burn the errors that these princes hold / Against her maiden truth" in Act 4 Scene 1. He devises a clever plan to restore Hero's good name and make Claudio feel remorseful. While Beatrice and Benedick help to recover Hero's honour, it is ultimately the Friar's wisdom which casts out the demons of despair and seals the happy ending with two marriages. Thus, religion is a moral instrument which exists in opposition to deceit.

Balthasar

Balthasar is one of Don Pedro's attendants, who sings the play's only song *Sigh No More*. You can read more about the song, and its significance on the following page of thematic analysis. Balthasar is modest about his musical ability, calling himself an "ill singer."

Section 5

Key Themes Analysis

Love and marriage

In the Renaissance tradition popularised by the sonnets of the 12th century Italian poet Petrarch, women were often portrayed as fickle and cold-hearted beauties with little in the way of personality. This was a source of anguish for the male lover, who pined after idealised notions of female beauty and unrequited love. In *Much Ado About Nothing,* Shakespeare inverts the Petrarchan dynamic through Balthasar's song *Sigh No More, Ladies:*

> QUOTES :
> "Sigh no more, Ladies, sigh no more,
> Men were deceivers ever,
> One foot in sea and one on shore,
> To one thing constant never."

Here, men are portrayed as the more fickle sex: between sea and shore, uncommitted to a single lover. The image of the sea, with its constantly shifting currents and tides, often symbolises mutability and transformation in Shakespeare – so it's a familiar metaphor for **protean** male love. Meanwhile, it is the ladies who "sigh," presumably with lovesick desire, following the example of the Petrarchan male hero.

Protean: tending to change frequently or easily.

This invites Shakespeare's audience to challenge their preconceived expectations about love and marriage. Although the play follows a traditional comedic narrative arch, where marriage forms the basis of a happy ending, many of our expectations about the way characters should behave are subverted along the way. Beatrice, with her bright intelligence and quick wit, is hardly a voiceless Petrarchan beloved: she is a woman who commands her own story rather than an object onto which male affection is projected.

Further, Beatrice and Benedick's relationship seems to go beyond mere adoration. Initially, they are opponents in a battle of wits and much of the language around their conversations recalls the war from which Benedick has returned. In the play's opening scene, Beatrice comments that "in our last conflict, four of his five wits went halting off," suggesting a military skirmish ("conflict") and the idea of wounds that made Benedick "hobble" (halt). Beatrice, then, is talking like a man, trespassing on the masculine world of war and wit, and it is this very characteristic that draws Benedick to her as an equal.

This early exchange also illustrates that Benedick and Beatrice are familiar with each other as friends (if not as lovers). Shakespeare juxtaposes this relationship with Claudio and Hero's younger, more naïve romance.

Lascivious:
lustful or
indecent.

Diana: the
Roman god of
childbirth,
fertility, and
chastity (as well
as hunting and
wild animals).

Binary:
opposition of
two contrasting
concepts.

Vignette: a
brief distillation
of an
experience; a
summary or
portrait of a
broader story.

Claudio's initial love for Hero is rather Petrarchan – he gushes that "in mine eye she is the sweetest lady I ever looked on" (Act 1 Scene 1). The word "eye" betrays the superficial nature of this love – the couple haven't had a single conversation yet. In fact, Claudio seems rather more in love with his image of Hero as a virginal beauty than with Hero herself. Perhaps this is why he is so easily taken in by the villains' ruse – Hero and Claudio's only face to face dialogue before the final scene occurs in Act 4 Scene 1, where he rails against Hero's "sign and semblance of honour" which hides what he perceives as **lasciviousness**. His narrative of Hero "as Dian in her orb" (comparing her to the virginal goddess **Diana**) has collapsed.

In archetypal comic tradition, *Much Ado About Nothing* is a play of **binaries** and patterns. The plot centres on the happy equilibrium of two couples. Don Pedro is flanked by two gallants, Don John by two mercenary villains. Messina is under the protection of two authorities, one military (Don Pedro) and one civil (Leonato). Two maids, Margaret and Ursula, attend the two noble ladies. These pairs interact with each other in a similar way to the dance in Act 2 Scene 1, where the audience is presented with a series of male/female conversations in the style of **vignettes**. Ultimately, it is the tension between, and among, the pairs which creates the conflict at the heart of the play and threatens to topple Messina's social order. When Hero's honour is restored, Shakespeare endorses marriage as a tool of resolution and harmony, the peak of fulfilment for young lovers. Those excluded from the joyous resolution are either too morose (Don John) or too stupid (Dogberry) to take part.

Gender and misogyny

When Beatrice bitterly exclaims "oh that I were a man!" (Act 4 Scene 1), she is expressing her resentment at her lack of agency in a world governed by gendered notions of honour and reputation. Male reputation, in Shakespeare's world, is derived from courage on the battlefield: Claudio is introduced to us as one who did "in the figure of a lamb, the feats of a lion" – a traditionally noble, warlike beast. Benedick, meanwhile, is described as a "good soldier," "stuffed with all honourable virtues." As young gallants returning from war, Benedick and Claudio represent aristocratic nobility and military honour. However, once they re-enter the domestic sphere of the home, Shakespeare calls traditional notions of masculinity into question – Benedick finds his equal in his "merry war" of wits with Beatrice and Claudio proves gullible and naïve.

By contrast, female reputation has an explicitly sexual dimension. The play's punning title alludes to this – in Elizabethan slang, a woman's 'O-thing' referred to her vagina, so *Much Ado About Nothing* refers to the scandal created when Hero's virginity is called into question. After Hero is apparently "done to death by slanderous tongues," the notion of female reputation becomes intertwined with life itself. For Hero, slander (or defamation) spells the 'death' of her marriage, her happiness, and the high regard in which she is held as a noble lady. This is, of course, a consequence which would be unimaginable for any of her male counterparts.

While Hero embodies the ideal of the chaste, dutiful daughter, Beatrice subverts masculine notions of feminine subservience through her sassy retorts. The pair can be described as foils for each other. From early in the play, Beatrice undermines Benedick's masculinity, calling him "no less than a stuffed man" in response to the messenger's praise of him. She is determinedly unmarried: she remarks that "I would rather hear my dog bark at a crow than a man swear he loves me." Hero, however, is meek, happily accepting her arranged marriage to Claudio with little awareness of her own powerlessness. Later in the play, Beatrice passionately defends her cousin's innocence. Her assertion that she would "eat [Claudio's] heart in the marketplace" recalls the stereotypical metaphor of women as devouring monsters – like the **Medea** of Greek tragedy, she embraces savagery and barbarism over conventional womanhood, determined to avenge her cousin's shame. This rage, however, is thwarted – she realises that "I cannot be a man with wishing, therefore I will die a woman with grieving."

Medea: a figure in Greek mythology who sought revenge on her unfaithful husband by murdering his new lover, and her own children.

In the male-dominated world of the play, Hero's claim to her innocence is worthless. For all her chastity and obedience, neither her father nor her fiance accept her version of events, indicating a broader misogynist conception of women as fickle and false. Beatrice, however, refuses to accept this. When she urges Benedick to "kill Claudio," perhaps the play's most shocking line, she forces Benedick to act on his belief in her cousin's innocence and take a stand against misogyny. Here, her undermining of his masculine qualities is more explicit: when Benedick initially refuses to kill his friend, she scoffs that "manhood is melted into curtsies." Thus, Beatrice reverses the conventional male-female dynamic: with the imperative "kill" she commands the power, while Benedick is made to feel feminine and weak. When, finally, he declares "enough, I am engaged, I will challenge him" he also goes against male ideals of military honour: he is willing to fight his fellow soldier, his companion on the battlefield.

Benedick's final words to Beatrice "peace I will stop your mouth" (presumably with a kiss) hint at a rapid sexual submission on her part after Hero's honour is restored – although this is clearly something she consents to. This is not to say Beatrice has merely become another submissive wife: unlike Hero, she has exercised agency in choosing her husband, and there is no pledge of obedience to Benedick. Nevertheless, Benedick talks on until the end of the play while Beatrice stays quiet: he impertinently tells the prince "get thee a wife," and proposes to punish Don John once the wedding celebrations are ended. This could be seen to suggest how little has changed – Beatrice's window of freedom is over and conventional gender norms are restored as the character's submit to the happy union of marriage.

Mistaken identity and disguise

As with many of Shakespeare's comedies, much of the confusion and conflict in the play is derived from mistaken identity or impersonation. In Act 2 Scene 1, Leonato welcomes his guests to Messina with a masque ball, which everyone attends in disguise. This scene can be interpreted as a microcosm of the world of the play: gossip is rife, no one is as they seem, and we are treated to a series of male/female interactions where each attempts to guess at the identity or the intention of the other.

When Don Pedro woos Hero on behalf of Claudio, she comments that "God defend the lute should be like the case," suggesting her hope that her would-be admirer is handsome beneath the grotesque masque he wears. Antonio claims to "counterfeit" himself when Ursula guesses at his true identity. Beatrice calls Benedick "the prince's jester, a very dull fool" to her dancing partner, who turns out to be Benedick himself. Within this comic ambience of erotic confusion, the audience is able to suspend their disbelief, accepting that characters do not recognise each other in masks and revelling in the comic potential of disguise.

After the dance, however, disguise takes on a darker dimension. Pretending to mistake Claudio for Benedick, Don John and Borachio suggest to him that Don Pedro wants Hero for himself. Here, the mask becomes the tool of villainy, a symbol for the villains' broader **obfuscation** of truth in an attempt to distort the romantic resolution which the audience expects.

Obfuscation: making something unclear or difficult to discern.

Later, mistaken identity becomes Hero's undoing when Margaret is mistaken for her when she lets Borachio in through Hero's window. Having seen the villains use disguise to their advantage, the audience is invited once again to suspend their disbelief. We are never informed where Hero was on that night, or why Beatrice, her "twelve month bedfellow," is unable to provide an alibi. In the **non-naturalistic** context of a comedy, however, this information proves irrelevant. As the play's master manipulator, Don John twists and engineers reality, creating the impression of infidelity where none exists – this is something the audience is bound to accept. When Claudio buys into this false narrative, chaos ensues and the apparently happy wedding is ruined.

Naturalistic: closely imitating real life (Shakespearean comedy plays are often non-naturalistic and will deliberately feature unrealistic timelines or plot points for the sake of the narrative).

This conflict is resolved through another counterfeit plot, albeit one where the truth is eventually revealed. Leonato presents a veiled Hero to Claudio as his niece, "almost the copy of my child that's dead." Here, Hero impersonates her living, untarnished self, while Claudio believes her to be disgraced and dead. She shows self-awareness of this ruse, commenting that "one Hero died defiled, but I do live." Once the veil is removed, sanity and reality are restored and the characters finally free themselves from the web of lies constructed by the villains.

Class and social order

In contrast to many of Shakespeare's other comedies, *Much Ado About Nothing* takes place in a real life location – Messina in Sicily – as opposed to an invented fantasy world. In the enclosed space of this small town, social norms, especially the class hierarchy, must be respected. As the governor of Sicily, Leonato has civil authority, yet he **defers** to Don Pedro, a prince and a conquering hero. In the opening scene, Leonato comments that "never came trouble to my house in the likeness of your grace," expressing a warm welcome towards Don Pedro as a visiting royal. Further, he expresses joy that no gentleman "of name" were lost in the wars, attaching a higher value to noble lives.

Defer: to submit or yield to someone else's superiority.

Don John, meanwhile, inhabits an uncertain place in the hierarchy. As the Prince's brother, he commands respect, but as a bastard, he is an automatic outsider. In Shakespeare's time, those known to be the product of illicit sex usually had no means of inheritance, so we can infer that Don John has had to rely on his own cunning. He is unwilling to embrace his brother's generosity, commenting that "I had rather be a canker in a hedge than a rose in his grace."

Unlike other characters, Beatrice and Benedick do not defer to this entrenched hierarchy. Their verbal sparring matches, rich in puns and wit, are reminiscent of the archetypal Elizabethan fool or court jester. Like jesters, they often use **hyperbole** to the point of ridicule – in Act 2 Scene 1, Benedick launches into a performance of exaggerated horror at the sight of Beatrice, mentioning increasing ludicrous locations ("the **Antipodes**," "the great Cham," "Prester John") where he might be sent to avoid her. In short, they do not behave how nobles are expected to behave, nor do they bow before Don Pedro's authority.

Hyperbole: exaggerations or overstatements.

Antipodes: Australia and New Zealand (a term often used in the northern hemisphere to refer to these places as being very far away!).

While neither Beatrice nor Benedick is rejected by the other noble characters, their friends' efforts to bring them "into a mountain of affection" are implicit attempts to make them fit into 'normal' society as a married couple. Their mutual disgust for marriage is alien to their aristocratic society and to the expectation that they will produce the next generation of lords and ladies. However, Benedick retains his signature disdain for authority until the play's end: he uses the familiar "thee" rather than the formal "you" with Don Pedro and suggests that it is he, and not the prince, who will "devise... brave punishments" for Don John.

The idiotic constable Dogberry doesn't make his appearance until Act 3; until this point, there has been no need for law enforcement. As head of the watch and protector of the city, he does not inspire confidence in the audience, foolishly instructing the watchmen that "the most peaceable way for you, if you do take a thief, is to let him show himself what he is and steal out of your company." In the topsy-turvy atmosphere of social confusion of the play, it is not surprising that the face of the law is incompetent and scatter-brained. After all, a competent police force would ruin the comic thrill of guessing if Dogberry will bungle the case. It is also worth noting that Dogberry is a lower-class character who lacks the self-awareness and social poise of the nobles.

However, even Shakespeare's treatment of young nobles Don Pedro and Claudio is not entirely sympathetic. Neither can love profoundly: as discussed above, Claudio's attachment to Hero is rather superficial and Don Pedro remains a solitary bachelor at the end of the play. When Claudio offers to accompany the Prince to Arragon immediately after his own wedding, Don Pedro comments that "nay, that would be as great a soil in the new gloss of your marriage as to show a child his new coat and forbid him to wear it." This simile suggests something rather childlike about Claudio: marriage is something to be tried on and flaunted like a new garment rather than taken seriously. Even their plan to bring Benedick

Solemnity:
being dignified and showing formal deference and respect.

and Beatrice together lacks **solemnity**, devised chiefly to satisfy their boredom while they wait for the wedding. In short, these young noblemen are portrayed as somewhat shallow in contrast to Benedick, not caring deeply for anything with the possible exception of battles.

Noting

The title *Much Ado About Nothing* puns on several alternative meanings. Taken literally, the title means that a scandal has been made over something insignificant. As explained above, it's also a clear double entendre based on the Elizabethan slang "o-thing", meaning vagina. Finally, "nothing" and "noting" were pronounced the same in Elizabethan English, so it can also be taken to mean that a scandal has been created over what characters have 'noted,' or overheard, and indeed failed to note. Beatrice and Benedick's romance is engineered by their friends through overheard conversations – they develop feelings based on what they 'notice'. Claudio notes Margaret, whom he believes to be Hero, at the window, and sabotages his own wedding as a result. As an outsider, Don John garners much of his information through spying and eavesdropping so he can turn the characters against each other.

The play takes place in a somewhat closed world: Messina is evidently a small community where everyone knows everyone's business. While Don Pedro is from Aragon, he is clearly a familiar figure in Messina from the warm welcome extended to him by Leonato. Gossip, then, is bound to be rife and the noble characters delight in using the power of rumour to bring Benedick and Beatrice together. Ironically, both are vulnerable to this type of manipulation as observant, sharp-witted characters. When Beatrice overhears Hero and Ursula exaggerating

Cagey:
reluctant to give information; being overly cautious or suspicious.

her disdainful manner and suggesting that she would scorn Benedick's love, she exclaims "contempt, farewell! And maiden pride adieu!" too proud to fulfil their mockery of her. However, it would be wrong to characterise the relationship as mere arranged 'noting' – another reason why both lovers are willing to believe each is smitten with the other is the atmosphere of **cagey** wooing which has existed between them since the beginning of the play.

Explicit references to noting abound in *Much Ado About Nothing*. For example, in Act 1 Scene 1, Benedick tells Claudio, "I noted [Hero] not, but I looked on her," implying that Hero is not worth his friend's attention as he tries to dissuade him from getting married. On a **meta-theatrical** level, the audience also plays a role in this 'noting' – the all-seeing audience perspective means we are always a step ahead of the characters in our 'noting'. For example, we have noted the details of Don John's scheme before anyone else in the play even realises something's wrong. You can find more examples of wordplay on 'noting' on page 37.

Meta-theatre: when a play contains dramatic or self-referential elements, drawing attention to the fact that it is a play.

Section 6

Structural Features Analysis

Plot structure

Like Shakespeare's other plays, *Much Ado About Nothing* is divided into five acts. The first two acts build both romantic and political intrigue: Claudio and Hero are engaged, Don Pedro brings Beatrice and Benedick into a "mountain of affection," and Don John schemes to humiliate his brother and ruin the upcoming wedding.

In Act 3, the respective schemes begin to come to fruition: Don John sows the fatal seeds of doubt in Claudio's mind and Beatrice and Benedick put aside their scorn for marriage.

The play reaches its climax at the beginning of Act 4. The wedding, which should be the play's resolution, the peak of comedic happiness, is sabotaged by the slander of Hero.

Denouement:
the final part of
a narrative
where all
characters are
brought
together, and
all strands of
the plot are
resolved.

In the remainder of Act 4 and Act 5, the action begins to de-escalate towards the play's **denouement**. Hero's shame is slowly revealed to be the result of malicious slander, Beatrice and Benedick finally admit their love for each other, and the villains are apprehended. Since this is a comedy, the resolution takes the form of a happy double wedding and the curtain closes on the characters merrily dancing together.

This plot structure is typical of a Shakespearean comedy and an Elizabethan audience would have been familiar with the dramatic conventions. A good way to think about this structure is to think of the climax (i.e. the aborted wedding scene) as the centre of the play. Everything surrounding it is either working towards it or resolving its aftermath.

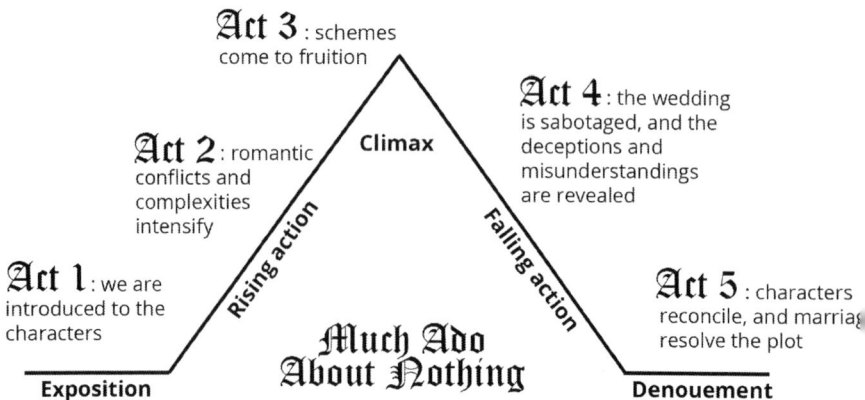

Act 3 : schemes come to fruition

Act 4 : the wedding is sabotaged, and the deceptions and misunderstandings are revealed

Act 2 : romantic conflicts and complexities intensify

Climax

Act 1 : we are introduced to the characters

Rising action

Act 5 : characters reconcile, and marriage resolve the plot

Falling action

Much Ado About Nothing

Exposition

Denouement

Verse

Verse, or poetry, is recognisable by its regular rhythm and can be rhymed or unrhymed (this is known as blank verse). Shakespeare typically follows a type of meter called iambic pentameter. Meter refers to the number of stressed (emphasised) and unstressed syllables per line. A line of iambic pentameter contains five unstressed syllables alternated with stressed syllables (known as iambs). For example, in Act 3 Scene 1, after Beatrice overhears Hero and Ursula discussing Benedick's "love" for her, she declares:

> QUOTES :
> "What **fire** is **in** my **ears**? Can **this** be **true**?
> Stand **I** con**demned** for **pride** and **scorn** so **much**?
> Con**tempt**, fare**well**, and **maiden** **pride**, a**dieu**,
> No **glory** **lives** be**hind** the **back** of **such**."

Here, we can observe a strong underlying rhythm in Beatrice's speech (with the bold syllabus being the stressed iambs), as well as alternately rhyming lines. Verse is often used to denote noble characters, especially in romantically-charged scenes. For example, the revelation of Benedick's love forces Beatrice to confront the reality of her own feelings for Benedick and abandon her scornful **façade**. This contrasts with her demeanour in earlier scenes, where she delivers sassy comebacks in prose and doesn't seem preoccupied with romance.

Façade: a deceptive outer appearance.

Prose

In contrast, prose usually denotes lower-class characters or alternatively comedic scenes. For example, although the scene where Benedick discovers that Beatrice "loves" him mirrors her later revelation, the tone is distinctly different. Whereas Beatrice's poetical declaration represents a serious crisis of identity, Benedick's scene is played for laughs. With Benedick, Shakespeare is pointing out the absurdity of a man who earlier mocked Claudio as "Monsieur Love" suddenly finding himself overcome by the same feeling, as in Act 2 Scene 3:

> QUOTES :
> **Benedict:** I will be horribly in love with her: I may chance have some odd quirks or remnants of wit broken on me, because I have railed so long against marriage: but doth not the appetite alter? A man loves the meat in his youth that he cannot endure in his age. Shall quips and sentences, these paper bullets of the brain awe a man from the career of his humour?

Stream of consciousness: the continuous flow of a person's thoughts, often expressed in literature in lengthy or ungrammatical ramblings.

Here, Benedick speaks in long, prose sentences broken by very few full stops and intermittent rhetorical questions. This creates more of a **stream of consciousness** feeling. It's also worth noting that Dogberry, the play's default 'fool', never speaks in verse. Despite his attempts to adopt a complex vocabulary, his lower class status is betrayed both by his constant use of malapropisms and his inability to speak in verse like the noble characters.

Stage directions

As with all Shakespeare plays, the stage directions in *Much Ado* are brief and mainly concerned with characters' entrances and exits. They do not, for example, describe *how* a particular character might dress, look or move, which gives modern directors room for creative interpretation. For example, in Act 2 Scene 3, when Benedick hides in the orchard, it's not clear whether there was an arbor prop on stage or whether he was merely hiding behind one of the stage pillars. Different stagings allow for different levels of comedy, depending on how convinced Benedick is that he cannot be seen or heard by those he eavesdrops on.

Symbolism and motifs

Bulls and horns

The motif of the cuckold's horns has appeared in literature since medieval times and seems to allude to the mating habits of stags, who forfeit their mates when defeated by another male. Throughout the play, references to horns and bulls reference the male characters' latent fears of cuckoldry, or sexual infidelity on the part of their wives.

For example (in Act 1 Scene 1), in response to Don Pedro's suggestion that he will one day get married, Benedick replies:

> QUOTES :
> **Benedict:** The savage bull may; but if ever the sensible
> Benedick bear it, pluck off the bull's horns and set
> them in my forehead: and let me be vilely painted,
> and in such great letters as they write 'Here is
> good horse to hire,' let them signify under my sign
> 'Here you may see Benedick the married man.'

Here, we see that Benedick views all married men as potential cuckolds. Getting married, then, would be tantamount to wearing the cuckold's horns on his forehead, thereby accepting **emasculation** and humiliation.

Emasculation: to deprive a man of his male role, power, or identity.

Dancing, doubles, and symmetry

Like a courtly dance, *Much Ado About Nothing* is a play of contrasts, parallels, patterns, and symmetry. The plot is not naturalistic but ritualistic. Don Pedro and Don John mirror each other as agents of good and evil; part of the play's suspense is which element will triumph over the other. Beatrice and Hero are two eligible young ladies and yet Shakespeare emphasises the contrast between them: Hero's traditional femininity vs. Beatrice's brazen sassiness. You can find more examples of doubling and twinning on page 28.

These recurring dual images bring to mind the **synchronisation** of two lovers dancing, reminding the audience that marriage, and presumably fertility, awaits each character (unless, of course, like Don John, they are too malevolent to find love). Early in the play, the masque ball scene provides an example of an actual courtly dance. In some ways, this scene can be read as a **microcosm** of the play as a whole: we see a series of short vignettes after which the characters "move on in the dance." Many of their conversations are about mistaken or counterfeit identity, foreshadowing Claudio's fatal mistake when he sees Margaret at Hero's window. The whole scene has an air of gossip and rumour. The structured nature of the dance also reflects the nobles adherence to the social hierarchy: Beatrice remarks that "if they lead to any ill, I will leave them at the next turning," embodying her disdain for societal expectation.

Synchronise: things occurring at the same time.

Microcosm: a miniature representation of a larger whole, encapsulating and distilling the important parts of the bigger picture.

Masks

At the masque ball, all the male characters appear in disguise (whether the women are also in masks varies from production to production). This image of hidden identity can be interpreted on multiple levels. On the surface, the masks conceal the characters' identities, which, as explained above, **portends** the case of mistaken identity upon which the plot hinges. Further, the masks allow the characters to overhear, or *note,* matters they would not otherwise have heard. For example, Benedick hears Beatrice describe him as "the prince's jester, a very dull fool" – although it's not clear whether she sees through his disguise. In any case, he responds to her not as Benedick but as a stranger at the ball; his mask shields him from her scorn. The masks also mirror the way the ball's atmosphere of joy and merriment hides the sinister plotting happening behind the scenes. As soon as the merry dance concludes, the villains come out of the shadows.

Portends: acts as a warning sign, omen, or foreshadowing of future calamitous events.

Poetry and songs

The play's first song, *Sigh No More,* bears a strong resemblance to a Petrarchan sonnet. However, it also parodies Petrarchan love by reversing the gender roles: it is the ladies who "sigh," presumably with lovesick desire, while the men are inconstant and fickle – "one foot in sea and one on shore." Balthasar, the singer, is supposedly a poor musician: Benedick comments that "he had been a dog that would have howled thus, I would have hanged him." It's therefore unclear whether the song is supposed to be taken seriously or whether it's merely part of the general merrymaking which characterises comedic plotlines.

The "solemn hymn" sung at Hero's false tomb is in the style of a traditional **lament**. Hero is called "virgin knight," a mythological allusion which links her to Diana, the virginal goddess of the hunt who surrounded herself with virgin followers. The alternating rhymes of the last few lines maintain the scene's ceremonial quality, while the repetition of "heavily" suggests the burden of Claudio's guilt and grief over Hero's apparent death.

Lament: a passionate expression of grief or sorrow.

Epitomise: to be a perfect example of something.

Benedick, meanwhile, is an inadequate sonnet writer. When trying in vain to compose a sonnet for Beatrice, Benedick comments that "I was not born under a rhyming planet, nor I cannot woo in festival terms." This **epitomises** his rejection of overblown, superficial Petrarchan love and distinguishes him from Claudio and his "very fantastical banquet" of words in praise of Hero.

Linguistic devices

Malapropisms

The bumbling character of Dogberry embodies the comic nature of mistaken identity through his constant use of malapropisms – using one word when he means another, similar sounding word. For example, in Act 3 Scene 3, he calls George Seacoal "the most *senseless* and fit man for the constable of the watch." Ironically, Seacoal could be described as senseless: like the rest of the watch, he is clearly an amiable fool, although this clearly isn't what Dogberry means. In this way, words are much like people and identities – one can easily be mistaken for another.

Metaphor and simile

Metaphor and simile are both recurring figures of speech in *Much Ado About Nothing*. For example, in Act 3 Scene 1, Hero remarks to Ursula "for I know [Beatrice's] spirits are coy and wild / As haggards of the rock". A haggard is a female hawk reared in the wild (as opposed to hand-reared and trained for hunting). This suggests Beatrice's stubborn, independent nature in contrast to Hero's willing filial obedience.

At the aborted wedding, Claudio tells Leonato "give not this rotten orange to your friend." This metaphor evokes the imagery of an orange which looks fresh and ripe on the outside and is spoiled within – just as Claudio believes Hero to be a "common stale" masquerading as a virgin.

Typically, similes and metaphors plant a vivid mental image in the audience's mind, adding colour to the characters' dialogue and emphasising certain observations.

Mythological allusions

Much Ado About Nothing contains numerous examples of allusions (or references) to Greco-Roman mythology. For example, in Act 4 Scene 1, Claudio says to Hero "You seem to me as Dian in her orb... But you are more intemperate in your blood/ Than Venus" Diana, or Dian, the Roman goddess of the hunt, was eternally chaste, while Venus, the goddess of love, was seen as the epitome of lust and sensuality. Later, Hero is referred to as "virgin knight" – a follower of Diana. These two allusions emphasise Hero's almost divine purity, making the slander against her even more tragic.

Punning and wordplay

Like all Shakespeare plays, *Much Ado About Nothing* contains numerous examples of punning and wordplay, especially in Benedick and Beatrice's verbal sparring matches. For example, in Act 2 Scene 1, Beatrice tells the disguised Benedick "I am sure [Benedick] is in the fleet, I would he had boarded me." This continues a running **nautical** metaphor where the women, with their dresses flowing like sails, are the ships, while the men handle and "board" them. This could also be a pun on the **homonym** "bawd" – a woman in charge of a brothel – suggesting the sexual tension between the two characters.

This witty (and sometimes bawdy) wordplay recalls the archetypal Elizabethan fool, suggesting that Beatrice and Benedick are not typical nobles but rather more intelligent and less adherent to social norms.

Nautical: things related to sailing, the sea, or ocean navigation.

Homonym: two words that sound the same but are spelled differently and have different meanings.

Section 7

Quote Bank

Love and marriage

Quote	Character	Act/Scene
"It is certain that I am loved of all ladies, only you [Beatrice] excepted: and I would I could find in my heart that I had not a hard heart, for truly I love none."	Benedick	Act 1 Scene 1
"I had rather hear my dog bark at a crow than a man swear he loves me."	Beatrice	Act 1 Scene 1
"Is't come to this? In faith, hath not the world one man, but he will wear his cap with suspicion? Shall I never see a bachelor of three score again? Go to, i'faith, and thou [Claudio] wilt needs thrust thy neck into a yoke, wear the print of it, and sigh away Sundays."	Benedick	Act 1 Scene 1
"Because I will not do [women] the wrong to mistrust any, I will do myself the right to trust none and the fine is (for the which I will live the finer) I will live a bachelor."	Benedick	Act 1 Scene 1
"But now I am returned, and that war-thoughts / Have left their places vacant, in their rooms / Come thronging soft and delicate desires, / All prompting me how fair young Hero is, / Saying I liked her ere I went to wars."	Claudio	Act 1 Scene 1
"I had rather be a canker in a hedge, than a rose in his grace, and it better fits my blood to be disdained of all, than to fashion a carriage to rob love from any."	Don John	Act 1 Scene 3
"Well, niece, I hope to see you one day fitted with a husband."	Leonato	Act 2 Scene 1
"Not til God make men of some other metal than earth: would it not grieve a woman to be overmastered with a piece of valiant dust?"	Beatrice	Act 2 Scene 1

"Friendship is constant in all things, / Save in the office and affairs of love: / Therefore all hearts in love use their own tongues. / Let every eye negotiate for itself. / And trust no agent: for beauty is a witch, / Against whose charms faith melteth into blood"	Claudio	Act 2 Scene 1
"Come, lady, you have lost the heart of Signor Benedick."	Don Pedro	Act 2 Scene 2
"Indeed, my lord, he lent it me a while, and I gave him use for it, a double heart for his single one: marry once before he won it of me, with false dice, therefore your grace may well say I have lost it."	Beatrice	Act 2 Scene 2
"If we can do this, Cupid is no longer an archer, his glory shall be ours, for we are the only love-gods."	Don Pedro	Act 2 Scene 1
"I do much wonder, that one man seeing how much another man is a fool, when he dedicates his behaviours to love, will after he hath laughed at such shallow follies in others, become the argument of his own scorn, by falling in love"	Benedick	Act 2 Scene 3
"I may chance have some odd quirks and remnants of wit broken on me, because I have railed so long against marriage: but doth not the appetite alter?"	Benedick	Act 2 Scene 3
"[Beatrice] cannot love, / Nor take no shape nor project of affection, / She is so self endeared."	Hero	Act 3 Scene 1
"And Benedick, love on, I will requite thee, / Taming my wild heart to thy loving hand: / If thou dost love, my kindness shall incite thee / To bind our loves up in a holy band"	Beatrice	Act 3 Scene 1
"But fare thee well, most foul, most fair, farewell / Thou pure impiety, and impious purity, / For thee I'll lock up the gates of love / And on my eyelids shall conjecture hang, / To turn all beauty into thoughts of harm."	Claudio	Act 4 Scene 1

Quote	Character	Act/Scene
"When [Claudio] shall hear she died upon his words / Th'idea of her life shall sweetly creep / Into his study of his imagination, / And every lovely organ of her life, / Shall come apparelled in more precious habit"	Friar	Act 4 Scene 1
"By my sword, Beatrice, thou lovest me... I will swear by it that you love me, and I will make him eat it that says I love not you"	Benedick	Act 4 Scene 1
"Sweet Hero, now thy image doth appear, / In the rare semblance which I loved it first."	Claudio	Act 5 Scene 1
"Thou and I are too wise to woo peaceably"	Benedick	Act 5 Scene 2
"And when I lived I was your other wife, / And when you loved, you were my other husband."	Hero	Act 5 Scene 4

Gender and misogyny

Quote	Character	Act/Scene
"In our last conflict, four of [Benedick's] five wits went halting off, and now is the whole man governed with one"	Beatrice	Act 1 Scene 1
"He were an excellent man that were made just in the mid way between [Don John] and Benedick: the one is too like an image and says nothing, and the other too like my lady's eldest son, evermore tattling."	Beatrice	Act 2 Scene 1
"By my troth, niece, thou wilt never get thee a husband if thou be so shrewd of thy tongue."	Leonato	Act 2 Scene 1
"It is my cousin's duty to make curtsy and say, father, as it please you: and yet for all that, cousin, let him be a handsome fellow, or else make another curtsy and say, father, as it please me."	Beatrice	Act 2 Scene 1
"Count, take of me my daughter, and with her my fortunes"	Leonato	Act 2 Scene 1
"Sigh no more, ladies, sigh no more / Men were deceivers ever, / One foot in sea and one on shore, / To one thing constant never."	Balthasar	Act 2 Scene 3

"But nature never framed a woman's heart, / Of prouder stuff than that of Beatrice: / Disdain and scorn ride sparkling in her eyes, / Misprising what they look on"	Hero	Act 3 Scene 1
"if you love [Hero], then tomorrow wed her, but it would better fit your honour to change your mind."	Don John	Act 3 Scene 2
"God give me joy to wear it, for my heart is exceeding heavy."	Hero	Act 3 Scene 4
"'Twill be heavier soon for the weight of a husband."	Margaret	Act 3 Scene 4
"There, Leonato, take [Hero] back again, / Give not this rotten orange to your friend, / She's but the sign and semblance of her honour, / Behold how like a maid she blushes here!"	Claudio	Act 4 Scene 4
"Oh fate! Take not away thy heavy hand, / Death is the fairest cover for [Hero's] shame, / That may be wished for."	Leonato	Act 4 Scene 1
"Is he not approved in the height a villain, that hath slandered, scorned, dishonoured my kinswoman? O that I were a man! What, bear her in hand until they come to take hands; and then, with public accusation, uncovered slander, unmitigated rancour, O God, that I were a man! I would eat his heart in the market-place."	Beatrice	Act 4 Scene 1
"Princes and counties! Surely, a princely testimony, a goodly count, Count Comfect; a sweet gallant, surely! O that I were a man for his sake! or that I had any friend would be a man for my sake! But manhood is melted into courtesies, valour into compliment, and men are only turned into tongue, and trim ones too: he is now as valiant as Hercules that only tells a lie and swears it. I cannot be a man with wishing, therefore I will die a woman with grieving."	Beatrice	Act 4 Scene 1

Quote	Character	Act/Scene
"You [Claudio] are a villain, I jest not, I will make it good how you dare with what you dare, and when you dare: do me right, or I will protest your cowardice: you have killed a sweet lady and her death shall fall heavy on you."	Benedick	Act 5 Scene 1

Mistaken identity and disguise

Quote	Character	Act/Scene
"I cannot hide what I am: I must be sad when I have cause and smile at no man's jests: eat when I have stomach, and wait for no man's leisure, sleep when I am drowsy, and tend on no man's business: laugh when I am merry, and claw no man in his humour."	Don John	Act 1 Scene 3
I know you well enough, you are Signor Antonio... I know you by the waggling of your head."	Ursula	Act 2 Scene 1
"At a word, I am not... To tell you true, I counterfeit him."	Antonio	Act 2 Scene 1
"Thus answer I in the name of Benedick, /But hear these ill news with the ears of Claudio"	Claudio	Act 2 Scene 1
"Out on thy seeming, I will write against it! / You seem to me as Dian in her orb, / As chaste as is the bud ere it be blown: / But you are more intemperate in your blood, / Than Venus, or those pampered animals, / That rage in savage sensuality."	Claudio	Act 4 Scene 1
"Would the two princes lie, and Claudio lie, / Who loved her so, that speaking of her foulness, / Washed it with tears?"	Leonato	Act 4 Scene 1
"One Hero died defiled but I do live, / And surely as I live, I am a maid."	Hero	Act 5 Scene 4

Class and social order

Quote	Character	Act/Scene
How many gentleman have you lost in this action?... A victory is twice itself, when the achiever brings home full numbers."	Leonato	Act 1 Scene 1
"Never came trouble to my house in the likeness of your grace: for trouble being gone, comfort should remain: but when you depart from me, sorrow abides, and happiness takes his leave."	Leonato	Act 1 Scene 1
"[Leonarto has] no child but Hero, she's his only heir."	Don Pedro	Act 1 Scene 1
"The fault will be in the music, cousin, if you be not wooed in good time: if the prince be too important, tell him there is measure in everything, and so dance out the answer."	Beatrice	Act 2 Scene 1
"We must follow the leaders... if they lead to any ill, I will leave them at the next turning."	Beatrice	Act 2 Scene 1
"Unless I might have another for working days, your grace is too costly to wear every day"	Beatrice	Act 2 Scene 1
"If he will not stand when he is bidden, he is none of the prince's subjects."	Verges	Act 3 Scene 3
"True, and they are to meddle with none but the prince's subjects: you shall also make no noise in the streets, for, for the watch to babble and to talk, is most tolerable and not to be endured."	Dogberry	Act 3 Scene 3
"This man said, sir, that Don John the prince's brother was a villain."	Seacoal	Act 4 Scene 2
"Write down, Prince John a villain, why this is flat perjury to call a prince's brother villain."	Dogberry	Act 4 Scene 2
"My lord, for your many courtesies I thank you: I must discontinue your company, your brother the bastard is fled from Messina, you have among you killed a sweet and innocent lady"	Benedick	Act 5 Scene 1

Noting

Quote	Character	Act/Scene
"Benedick, didst thou note the daughter of Signor Leonato?"	Claudio	Act 1 Scene 1
"I noted her not, but I looked on her."	Benedick	Act 1 Scene 1
"Nay pray thee, come; / Or if thou wilt hold longer argument, / Do it in notes."	Don Pedro	Act 2 Scene 3
"Note this before my notes: / There's not a note of mine that's worth the noting."	Balthasar	Act 2 Scene 3
"Why, these are very crotchets that he speaks – Note notes, forsooth, and nothing!"	Don Pedro	Act 2 Scene 3
"For look where Beatrice like a lapwing runs / Close to the ground, to hear our conference."	Hero	Act 3 Scene 1
"You are to bid any man stand, in the Prince's name.... Why then take no note of him, but let him go."	Dogberry	Act 3 Scene 3
"Thou knowest that the fashion of a doublet, or a hat, or a cloak is nothing to a man."	Borachio	Act 3 Scene 3
"Hear me a little, / For I have only been silent so long / And given way unto this course of fortune / By noting of the lady."	Friar Francis	Act 4 Scene 1

Section 8

Sample Essays

Essay One

QUESTION: How do male and female notions of honour differ in *Much Ado About Nothing?*

ESSAY	COMMENTS
INTRODUCTION In *Much Ado About Nothing,* Shakespeare interrogates gendered notions of honour within the context of a hierarchical society preoccupied with reputation.[1] While male honour is derived from military feats and masculine comradery, women are almost exclusively defined by their sexual fidelity and their ability to be possessed by men.[2] The tension between these differing notions of honour culminates in Beatrice's frustrated exclamation that "men are only turned into tongue," as she mocks masculine conceptions of chivalry and forces Benedick to stand against the misogyny which threatens the innocent Hero.	1. From the very first sentence, this essay is directly engaging with the prompt, and building upon the idea of honour and gender together. A common mistake students make is attempting to only explore key words in isolation, rather than acknowledging the entire message within the prompt. 2. We then expand upon our contention by explaining the differences between male and female conceptions of honour, and relating this to the specifics of the text before commencing with our first sub-argument.

PARAGRAPH 1

Initially, Hero's character serves as a foil for Beatrice, an honourable counterpart to her cousin's rebellious offending against societal convention.[3] In the opening scene, Hero speaks only one line, which clarifies Beatrice's mocking of Benedick as "Signor Mountanto" – her silence amplifies her cousin's sassy, argumentative demeanour. When Hero is betrothed to Claudio, she is passed like a voiceless commodity[4] from Leonato to Don Pedro. Indeed, Leonato's line "take of me my daughter and with her my fortunes" barely elevates Hero beyond the status of a chattel; love is subordinate to economic and cultural considerations. It is Beatrice who attempts to return some of Hero's agency when she tells her "speak, cousin, or (if you cannot) stop his mouth with a kiss and let him not speak neither." Nevertheless, critical characterisation of Hero as a nonentity is overly simplistic.[5] In Act 3 Scene 1, where she prepares to gull Beatrice in the orchard, Hero uses a series of imperatives – "run", "whisper," "say," "bid"[6] – hinting at a resourceful side to her character which has hitherto been hidden. A model maiden, Hero has become acculturated to men speaking for her or about her and demurs to them for the sake of her reputation. With her female companions, however, she is confident, ingeniously playing on her cousin's "self-endeared" nature.

3. Try to avoid ever having one body paragraph focused on only one character, as some of the best analysis happens when you are able to compare and contrast characters.

4. Already we are making insightful comments about the significance of Hero's character, and her role in the play.

5. This marks an important shift in our argument, as we discuss an alternate view of Hero's character that considers how she does have some agency and honour, even if her capacity to express this is impaired by the social conventions of the time.

6. Remember that you can group similar quotes together and analyse them collectively – this can make for highly sophisticated and efficient analysis!

PARAGRAPH 2

The cruel ease with which Hero's spotless reputation is soiled and slandered hints at the devaluation of a woman's word – whether or not she conforms to social expectation.[7] While Leonato admonishes the boisterous Beatrice that "thou wilt never get thee a husband, if thou be so shrewd of thy tongue," it is the mild, gentle[8] Hero who is denounced as a "rotten orange" and a "common stale." Moreover, in the aborted wedding scene, Claudio's oxymoronic talk of "pure impiety, and impious purity" exposes the sheer absurdity of his accusations and the ease with which female honour crumbles under the weight of masculine scorn. Even Leonato,[9] a supposedly loving father, immediately wishes his daughter dead rather than tarnished as a whore. Hero's apparent "death," then, is not merely counterfeit but a symbolic representation of the death of her honour at the hands of the patriarchy. Herein lies the tragedy of female honour: Shakespeare shows his audience that even the paragon virgin may find herself shamed as one who "knows the heat of a luxurious bed," her own truth overshadowed by male dishonesty.[10]

7. This topic sentence furthers the ideas conveyed in the previous paragraph while also tying in the concepts of gender differences implied by the prompt, and sets the foundation for a discussion of *dishonour*. This might not be an immediately obvious sub-topic to explore for this essay question, but brainstorming and planning can help you discover more unique ideas like this.

8. Note that many mentions of characters here are accompanied by adjectives to describe their characteristics, thereby quickly conveying our holistic understanding of the play.

9. This paragraph effectively analyses Hero, Leonato, and Claudio, combining a fluent discussion of all of them to lead to the overwhelming paragraph conclusion.

10. This is a powerful analysis of this theme, and conveys an overarching interpretation at the crucial moment of the paragraph ending. These are your opportunities to show your assessor how well you know the text, and how strong your contention is.

PARAGRAPH 3

Male honour, by contrast, is far more securely rooted in military tradition and masculine friendship. Just as Hero dies by her reputation, Claudio lives through his: in the opening scene, he is praised for "doing in the figure of a lamb the feats of a lion." Within the domestic sphere, Claudio's behaviour is somewhat passive and inadequate, perhaps better suited to the proverbial lamb. However, having earned the affection of Don Pedro, a military authority figure, he maintains his reputation as an honourable young gallant – a reputation he strives to protect. Before he decides to woo Hero, he asks Benedick "is she not a modest young lady?" His affection, then, is not a true upwelling of romantic desire[11] but an attraction built on concern for his reputation and a desire to embody the role of the virile patriarch rather than the cuckold. Indeed, Don John exploits Claudio's obsession with reputation when he tells him "if you love [Hero], then tomorrow wed her: but it would better fit your honour to change your mind."[12] While he urges Claudio to trust the "evidence" of his own eyes, the mere mention of honour between men is conveyed by Shakespeare as being enough to plant doubt in Claudio's mind.

11. Notice how here we acknowledge a potential alternate interpretation, but then follow that up with our own reading of Claudio and cement this as a more justifiable view of the text. This showcases our ability to treat the text as a construct, which the audience can interpret in different ways, but still express our contention and back it up with evidence. This is exactly what the markers want to see! As such, it's worth including analysis like this at least once or twice in every essay.

12. Try to avoid ending a paragraph with a quote; as aforementioned, the ends of your body paragraphs should be the moments you explicitly convey the significance of this discussion to your assessor, and concluding a discussion with evidence might make it seem as though you have not been able to bring the analysis back to the core argument in your own words.

13. It's also a good idea to use Shakespeare's name at the ends of your paragraphs, as this forces you to zoom out and make broader statements about the meaning of the examples you have chosen.

PARAGRAPH 4

With Hero condemned and slandered, Beatrice's proto-feminist rage[14] erupts into speech as she urges Benedick to avenge her cousin. The bald command to "Kill Claudio" represents her disdain for chivalric notions of honour; she spurns the platonic bond Benedick shares with Claudio. When he initially refuses, she critiques male notions of honour as shallow and weak: "manhood is melted into curtsies, valour into compliment." The alliterative[15] references to "curtsies" and "compliment" suggest something feminine about false male bravado, hinting at the hypocrisy of male superiority. Beatrice also acknowledges her own powerlessness within this patriarchal world, declaring that "I cannot be a man with wishing, therefore I will die a woman with grieving." Benedick, then, becomes her instrument, a man who may carry the force of her revenge. His acceptance of this task represents a rejection of military comradery in favour of a new, truer notion of honour. Where before he delighted in bantering with his friends,[16] his challenge to Claudio is bare and pointed: "you have killed a sweet lady, and her death shall weigh heavy on you". After bearing his challenge, he promptly departs, dismissing Claudio as a mere "boy" and coolly rejecting Don Pedro's noble "company." By placing Hero's honour above his own duty to his commanding officer and fellow soldier, Benedick challenges the legitimacy of Messina's entrenched misogyny.

14. There are no set rules about how many body paragraphs you should write. Three or four is the norm, and I have chosen to write four here because this prompt is quite broad and requires a discussion of lots of different concepts. Alternatively, if this were a more basic prompt like 'Discuss the importance of honour in *Much Ado About Nothing*,' I might have instead focused on three sub-arguments and spent more time delving into those. Just make sure you strike a balance between depth and breadth, and that you are able to write a sufficient amount within the time constraints of your assessment task or exam.

15. Here, I'm closely examining the language and unpacking the significance of Shakespeare's word choices. It's always particularly impressive if you can demonstrate a range of analytical abilities, from analysing big things like character motivations to small things like the connotations or techniques embedded in individual words.

16. This analysis draws a distinction between how Benedick acts at different stages of the play, thereby allowing us to analyse his character trajectory and emotional growth.

CONCLUSION

Adhering to comic archetypes, Shakespeare[17] diverts the plot towards its expected romantic resolution and away from the troubling possibility of Claudio and Benedick killing each other in combat. Indeed, Benedick's final line to Beatrice "Peace, I will stop your mouth" suggests a return to conventional gender roles, where the woman sexually and emotionally submits to her husband. The contrast between the two couples, however, remains: even the most shallow observer can see that Benedick and Beatrice have far more to say to each other than Claudio and Hero. This love,[18] Shakespeare suggests, is built on a novel, shared conception of honour which goes beyond hollow notions of male chivalry and female chastity.

17. Your conclusion should always centre around the bigger picture of authorial intent. What is Shakespeare trying to say about the key ideas in this prompt (i.e. in this case, gender and honour)? If you can answer this question, your conclusion will have done its job!

18. You may also wish to zoom out to even broader ideas – what is Shakespeare saying about humanity, society, and emotions like love or ideals like honour? This is tricky to do, especially early in your studies where you may now have encountered these questions before, but with practice, it is guaranteed to make for an impressive final note for your essays.

Essay Two

QUESTION: "She's but the sign and semblance of her honour,
Behold how like a maid she blushes here!" (Claudio, Act 4 Scene 1)
In *Much Ado About Nothing,* the central problem is the characters' failure
to see beyond outward appearances. Discuss.

ESSAY	COMMENTS
INTRODUCTION From the amiable erotic confusion of the masque ball to Don John's deceitful schemes, morally ambiguous disguise[1] is central to the gossiping world of Messina. An inimical malcontent, Don John exploits Claudio's latent fear of cuckoldry and Leonato's casual misogyny, manipulating the bonds between the signifier and the signified. Shakespeare distinguishes between Claudio's purely superficial attraction and the novel, self-aware romance which blossoms between Benedick and Beatrice. With sharp-witted vivacity, Benedick and Beatrice interrogate the blind assumptions which mislead the other characters and are able to see beyond mere "seeming."	1. Notice how we have expanded on the prompt by introducing key words that are *implied,* but not directly given to us? This prompt might seem overly complicated at first, until you break it down and realise it is essentially asking you to talk about the theme of disguise. There are other facets we must consider, including the quote, but the most important starting point is to find the 'core' of the prompt, and then constructing a thesis or contention around this.

PARAGRAPH 1

Superficial and passive, Claudio reflects the archetypal Petrarchan lover[2] in his lack of agency and preoccupation with the female image. Enchanted by the sight of Hero, he exclaims to Benedick "in mine eye, she is the sweetest lady that ever I looked on." Here, the assonance of "mine" and "eye" draws attention to the visual nature of Claudio's language: it is the roving, superficial eye which is entrapped by Hero's beauty and not, presumably, the heart or the soul.[3] Later, after he is duped into thinking Don Pedro is wooing Hero for himself, he declares "Let every eye negotiate for itself." Again, the "eye" is the agent of desire, the negotiator which would broker a love-match. There is a certain irony in this melancholy speech: Claudio says he will no longer trust outward appearances, misogynistically characterising beauty as a mercurial "witch." However, he is falling headlong for the shadowy reality engineered by the villains, thereby failing to see the truth. Later, his sibilant assertion that Hero is "but the sign and semblance of her honour" once again reflects this painful naïvety: Claudio looks past Hero's true, virginal form toward the imaginary stains on her honour.

2. Remember: the assessors don't want to read an 'information dump' of all your background knowledge. Using words like 'Petrarchan lover' can be valuable in analysing Claudio's character, for instance, but you need to convey your understanding of these contextual terms without needing to define them or explain their history. Assume your marker also knows what these mean (as they will be just as familiar with the play as you are!) and try to just use them in passing reference, with related terms and explanations to complement your knowledge. For example, here we have noted that Claudio is superficial, passive, and lacks agency because of his obsession with attaining women, all of which are elements of a stereotypical Petrarchan lover. Hence, the assessor will know that we understand the meaning of that label without us having to define it!

3. This is a great example of close analysis, delving into the symbolism and significance of word choice. Obviously you shouldn't do this for every quote, but incorporating this highly specific analysis a few times in every essay will definitely impress your reader!

PARAGRAPH 2

However,[4] Claudio's latent fear of cuckoldry is arguably as fatal as his superficiality. Images of horns, a traditional symbol of cuckoldry since medieval times, abound in the play: Benedick declares that if he ever gets married "pluck off the bull's horns, and set them in my forehead," hinting that all husbands are potential cuckolds. On the Elizabethan stage, mockery of cuckolds was common, a popular counter-discourse to the sanctified view of marriage presented by the church. For the hapless Claudio, however, the possibility of being cuckolded is palpable, a stark reminder of his own romantic ineptitude. Thus, the constructed "seeming" of Margaret at the window is believable for Claudio not simply because he is naïve but because it represents his most primal fear.[5] Don John's assertion that "I will disparage [Hero] no further, till you are my witnesses" plays on Claudio's fear, tempting him with proof of what he suspects, asking him to trust his own eyes rather than mere rumour. At the aborted wedding, the stumbling alliteration of Claudio's exclamation "Oh what men daily do, not knowing what they do!" seems to allude to husbands who are unknowingly cuckolded by unfaithful wives, tethered to women who, in Claudio's view, are no better than whores.

PARAGRAPH 3

Indeed, this masculine preoccupation with female reputation is as damaging as malignant illusion.[6] With the wedding in ruins, Leonato's initial thought is not for Hero but for his own reputation: in anguish, he asks "hath no man's dagger here a point for me?"

4. This may seem like a simple linking word, but it is an important addition that aids the fluency of the essay. You don't want your body paragraphs to sound like three or four completely separate, unrelated arguments. Rather, you want to give the impression that you are building your ideas higher and higher, creating a tower of an essay! Words like these express a connection across paragraphs, and also make things flow easier for the teacher reading your essay.

5. This is an important layer to Claudio's character that some students may miss. It also ties in nicely with this discussion of 'seeming,' and of both internal and external fears.

6. This is another strong inter-paragraph link that connects the discussion of our second body paragraph (masculine preoccupation with female reputation) with what we will go on to talk about in the third (malignant illusion).

Later, when Beatrice can provide no alibi, he asks "would the two princes lie, and Claudio lie / Who loved her so, that speaking of her foulness, / Washed it with tears?"[7] While the sequence of rhetorical questions hint at Leonato's uncertainty, his loyalty is not with his daughter but with the misogynistic cultural mores which idealise virginity and devalue a woman's word, an entrenched patriarchal worldview which Don John uses to his advantage. The image of Hero's "foulness" cleansed by Claudio's tears sets up a dichotomy between male righteousness and female shame – a notion rejected by Beatrice when she condemns male promises, suggesting that "men are only turned into tongue." While they are initially deceived by Don Pedro's elaborate matchmaking, Benedick and Beatrice are far less reliant on outward appearances, building a novel love on mutual self-awareness. In the opening scene, Benedick's apostrophising of Beatrice as "Lady Disdain" satirises the Petrarchan trope of the marble-breasted, aloof beloved. Later,[8] he mocks Claudio's overblown praise of Hero as a "very fantastical banquet," hinting at the performative and verbose nature of his friend's newfound romance. When Don Pedro and Claudio condemn Hero as a "common stale," Benedick is more circumspect, waiting to pass judgement until he hears Beatrice's view. While Beatrice can provide no alibi, her declaration that "Oh on my soul my cousin is belied" proves enough to sway him. In contrast to Claudio, for whom illusion and reality are indistinguishable,[9] Benedick places his faith in Beatrice's judgement: Hero cannot be unfaithful because Beatrice knows her to be chaste.

7. Typically, it's best to keep quotes short and sweet – not only are they easier to memorise like this, but they are also more precise, and allow you to highlight the exact moments of the text that support your argument. However, you may at times wish to include a longer quote in order to demonstrate a more complex example or idea. Just make sure you don't do this too often, as the majority of your body paragraphs should be dedicated to your own analysis.

8. This paragraph covers a range of different examples pertaining to the characters' perspectives of worth and value, but it all flows together nicely – notice how both the sentence structure and the ideas lead into one another.

9. This draws an explicit parallel between Benedick and Claudio in order to tie the paragraph together.

PARAGRAPH 4

While Shakespeare ultimately delivers the expected comic resolution,[10] a double wedding, he also uses the play's denouement to explore paradoxes of true love in contrast to the obscure world of deception. The women enter veiled and indistinguishable, hinting at the deindividuation of the Petrarchan beloved; the female form becomes an object onto which male affection is projected. Indeed, Claudio's racist assertion that "I'd hold my mind were [Hero] an Ethiop" harks back to his earlier preoccupation with outward appearance: he mourns his fiancee's beauty and seems to view marrying one less beautiful as a romantic penance. Hero's eventual unveiling, then, represents[11] the triumph of truth over deception, comedy over tragedy, life and love over death. Benedick and Beatrice, however, remain more self-aware: while they may claim to take one another "out of pity," to love each other "no more than reason," they are able to see beyond these outward emotional representations.

10. Treat every element of the text as the product of deliberate authorial intent! Don't just say 'the play has a comic ending' – say 'Shakespeare delivers an expected comic resolution.' This awareness of how the text has been constructed in order to convey meaning is vital in achieving a high score.

11. Consider the symbolism or representation of certain plot points. This can help you avoid simply retelling the story, and ensures you are analysing the significance of your evidence.

CONCLUSION

In *Much Ado About Nothing,* Shakespeare critiques the naïvety of the superficial Petrarchan lover through the contrasting pairs of lovers.[12] While misogyny and cuckoldry anxiety contribute to the problem plot, the central villainy is predicated upon the characters' failure to question what they see and how things seem.

12. This conclusion is concise, but communicates everything it needs to. Remember that you typically only need two or three sentences here, so don't spend too long on your conclusion, especially in exam conditions where your limited time is best spent refining body paragraphs.

Essay Three

QUESTION: Discuss how Shakespeare blends the comedic and the tragic in this play.

ESSAY	COMMENTS
INTRODUCTION While the gossiping, festive world of Shakespeare's Messina teems with comic archetypes, the narrative landscape is also populated with darker imagery, exposing the deceit and misogyny at the heart of noble society. The interplay between the lovers, while comic, also conjures the idea of a sexual battleground: Benedick comments that Beatrice "speaks poniards and every word stabs." Noting, initially a comic device, is twisted into an instrument of deceit by the villains. Hero's counterfeit death is, of course, the zenith of melancholic imagery, symbolising the tragic death of her reputation in a society preoccupied with female virginity.[1]	1. This introduction explores various threads from the prompt in order to cover both the comedic and tragic elements of *Much Ado*. You could also spend more time unpacking these words here, or alternatively, leave this for your body paragraphs where you can explain them in context and with reference to textual evidence.
PARAGRAPH 1 Early in the play, rumour and misunderstanding form the basis of a comic plot not unlike the modern romantic comedy. The mirroring eavesdropping scenes, in which Benedick and Beatrice are each gulled into believing the other loves them, provide scope for a range of comic pratfalls.[2] For example, Hero mocks Beatrice's attempt to hide when she tells Ursula "for look where Beatrice like a lapwing runs / Close to the ground." Benedick's abrupt change of mind in regards to marriage is perhaps more comical: where before he viewed Beatrice as a woman "possessed with a fury," he now sees "marks of love" in her sassy behaviour. Here, rumour and overheard information become the Cupid's arrows of Don Pedro and his fellow "love gods" – to the presumed delight of the audience.[3]	2. Try to avoid taking words like 'comedic' for granted. It's not enough to just use this word and move on with your discussion – you should stop and explain how and why something is constructed in a comedic way, as shown here. 3. This is a relatively short first paragraph, but it efficiently imparts a strong grasp on what makes *Much Ado* a comedy, with close analysis of character behaviour, and references to likely audience interpretation. Later, as our arguments get more complex, the paragraphs will be slightly longer.

PARAGRAPH 2

Nevertheless, the proliferation of militaristic language in Beatrice and Benedick's dialogue evokes a darker view of romance and sexuality.[4] In the opening scene, Beatrice tells Benedick "nobody marks you," suggesting the idea of military marksmen and indicating Benedick's transition from a literal battleground to a sexual conflict. Army life and married life, then, can be read as two sides of the same coin: Benedick says of Claudio "he were wont to speak plain... like an honest man and a soldier and now he is turned orthography, his words are a very fantastical banquet." Here, the passive lover exists in opposition to the virile soldier and yet also embodies his ultimate destination: what young gallant doesn't seek a wife when he returns from war? Of course, the trope of the 'battle of the sexes' was popularly used to satirise marriage in Elizabethan England[5] and this scene initially seems to conform to comic archetypes. However, the verbal sparring, coupled with constant allusions to cuckoldry through the symbol of horns, also hints at a deep-seated fear of female sexuality. Later, when Benedick attempts to write a sonnet for Beatrice, the only rhymes he can find are "lady" and "baby," "scorn" and "horn," and "school" and "fool" – a troubling lexicon which connotes a husband cuckolded by his wife and forced to raise a bastard child. It is this latent fear, Shakespeare contends, which is exploited and eventually used to tarnish Hero's honour.[6]

4. This is a very good connecting topic sentence that links the previous discussion with the one to come.

5. This integration of contextual knowledge helps strengthen this point, but note that we don't spend more than half a sentence on this. The vast majority of your essay (if not all of it) should be focused exclusively on the text; only use background information if it contributes to your argument!

6. Towards the end of this paragraph, we start to build up towards an overarching point about Benedick's character, as well as a broader point about one of the more emotionally tragic parts of the play.

PARAGRAPH 3

Further, Shakespeare distorts the comedic device of 'noting' into something far more sinister as the villains' plot escalates towards its climax. Even the play's title[7] twists the notion of gossip into a double entendre: the word "nothing" can be read to mean "nothing," "noting," or "no-thing," Elizabethan slang for female genitalia; thus foreshadowing the dark controversy created around Hero's virginity. The matchbreaker to his brother's matchmaker, the villain Don John is himself a bastard, the product of illicit sex. The constructed appearance of Margaret as Hero at the window directly responds to the characters' constant noting, baiting Claudio into false supposition. Indeed, Don John tells Claudio to "bear it coldly til midnight, and let the issue show itself." Knowing he is not trusted, he does not ask for Claudio's confidence, instead using Don Pedro and Claudio's reliance on the overheard, the spied-upon, the surface level gossip, as well as their entrenched misogyny, to smear Hero's name.

7. This paragraph is a mini-banquet of analytical techniques! First we are discussing the structure of the plot, then linking this with some close analysis of the title's double meaning, which will then lead into a comparison of characters, all presented through the lens of the theme of 'noting.' Incorporating a range of devices and forms of evidence is a surefire way to impress your assessor!

PARAGRAPH 4

Upon hearing Claudio's condemnation of her, Hero's death-like faint symbolises not only her shock but also the murder of her reputation in the context of a Patriarchal society where women are seldom believed. The death of an innocent young woman is a common narrative trope in Shakespearean tragedies (for example, Ophelia in *Hamlet)* so even the appearance of death in a comedy is jarring, a palpable reminder of mortality in the midst of a wedding,[8] a celebration of fertility and life. Even the lexicon used to describe Hero becomes tainted: Leonato refers to her shame "printed in her blood," he laments that she is "fallen / Into a pit of ink." The coupling of "fallen" with "pit" suggests eternal damnation,[9] the punishment which he believes awaits his daughter in the next life. Later, when Claudio experiences remorse for Hero's apparent death, his "solemn hymn" is populated with tragic images, while the insistent chorus "Heavily, heavily" implies the burden of guilt that tortures his soul.

8. Here, we are acknowledging the blending of comedy and tragedy, and beginning to tie together our various sub-arguments.

9. This is another very good example of close analysis whereby we unpack the connotations of individual words. Including a quote and then pausing to examine some specific language within it can be an excellent way to showcase how deeply you've thought about the text.

CONCLUSION

The play's conclusion represents a return to comic archetypes in the form of a double wedding and the banishment of the villains from the narrative space. Hero is unveiled, living and sanctified, the embodiment of submissive female chastity. The curiously brief exchange of words between her and Claudio is somewhat perturbing for the attentive theatre-goer: can one really expect romantic bliss for this couple who have so little to say to each other? Shakespeare, however, leaves little time to ponder this, abruptly shifting the focus to Benedick and Beatrice. The pipers are ordered to "strike up" a merry jig and no one seems worried about the malcontent John; his punishment can be delayed as the couples savour their newfound happiness.[10]

10. Because this prompt focuses more so on specific elements of the text, this conclusion explains the importance of these in terms of the characters and the overall atmosphere of the play. It also briefly incorporates some evidence that was not in the body paragraphs – this is risky, and the safest option is usually to have your conclusion centre solely on themes and authorial intent, but you may find this to be an interesting alternative that lets you round off your discussion with some impressive insights about the play.

Essay Four

QUESTION: To what extent does Shakespeare endorse Messina's social order?

ESSAY	COMMENTS
INTRODUCTION In *Much Ado About Nothing,* the insular, almost claustrophobic atmosphere of Messina, where eavesdropping is rife and marriages are engineered through 'noting,' is governed by an obdurate social hierarchy not unlike that of Elizabethan England.[1] While civil and military authorities Leonato and Don Pedro are fundamentally benevolent figures, Shakespeare questions the legitimacy of this social order[2] by setting Claudio's blind obedience to social convention against the irreverent, clown-like figures of Beatrice and Benedick. Marriage, while ostensibly blissful, is also an instrument with which the would-be lovers can be reconciled to their expected social roles and a way of subordinating women.[3]	1. This opening sentence establishes the play's title, the setting, the plot, the social structure, and some contextual information (as well as, most importantly, a link to the prompt!). 2. If you find it difficult to establish a clear contention for your essay, or if your teacher tells you your contentions are not obvious enough, try to use an overt statement like this that explicitly answers the prompt's question in terms of Shakespeare's intention. 3. This is a good example of a closely related idea that isn't obviously a part of the prompt on first glance, but is an undoubtedly relevant foundation for our argument.

PARAGRAPH 1

Shakespeare warns[4] against complete subordinacy to one's social superiors through Claudio, who blindly follows Don Pedro to the detriment of his own agency. While he is introduced as a conquering hero, one who is celebrated for doing "in the figure of a lamb the feats of a lion," Claudio is far less experienced on the domestic battleground upon which he finds himself. Don Pedro's offer to woo Hero on his behalf, then, seems natural; Claudio tells his friend "how sweetly you do minister to love / That know's loves grief by his complexion!" While this remark clearly indicates respect for Don Pedro's worldliness, the word "minister" connotes religious authority, intimating that the Prince has some superior connection to love as a result of his noble birth.[5] The power imbalance in this scene would have been more visible to an Elizabethan audience: Don Pedro constantly reminds Claudio of his power and status by using the familiar *thee*,[6] Claudio defers to the Prince by respectfully addressing him as *you*. Inevitably, Claudio's class anxiety makes him an inept lover: even his betrothal occurs as a transaction between Don Pedro and Leonato. It is Beatrice who prompts Claudio to respond with the imperative "speak, Count, 'tis your cue."[7] The fact that Claudio has to be prompted by a woman hints at his emasculation under the rigid class norms he does not seek to question.

4. Ideally, your topic sentences should start with a bigger picture idea, such as what Shakespeare warns against, and then zoom in to a more specific detail in the play, such as a character's role in relation to others.

5. As always, if you have to include a longer quote of two or more lines of dialogue, having your next sentence dedicated to explaining it and picking out the one or two words that are most important will ensure your assessor doesn't just see this as summarising the plot.

6. This is an important stylistic feature of Shakespeare's plays, and can be a useful supplementary point when you are including a quote in which characters refer to one another as either "you" or "thee."

7. Note how this paragraph smoothly transitioned between quotes and analysis? This is typical of high-range pieces, so emulating this in your own work is almost guaranteed to improve your marks!

PARAGRAPH 2

Like the archetypal Elizabethan fool, Benedick and Beatrice subvert social norms through searing wit and scorn for the institution of marriage. In contrast to the other characters, whose dialogue veers between sentimental blank verse and workmanlike prose, Benedick and Beatrice's conversations are verbal sparring matches where clever puns are flung back and forth like daggers. Even Beatrice's nickname for Benedick 'Signor Mountanto' seems to ridicule his skill as a swordsman through its allusion to fencing terminology.[8] According to contemporary dramatic convention, this kind of dialogue should belong to a court jester; noble characters were far more often serious and sombre. While Benedick is undoubtedly the Prince's comrade, any servility he expresses is in satire. For example, wishing to avoid Beatrice's company, Benedick asks Don Pedro "will your Grace command me any service to the world's end?" and embarks upon a hyperbolic fantasy of errands he might run. The lexicon of far-flung places and peoples[9] – "the furthest inch of Asia," "the Great Cham's beard," "the pygmies" – is reminiscent of the mock learning which was typical of Elizabethan fooling. It is unsurprising then, that both Benedick and Beatrice scorn marriage: Benedick mocks husbands as cuckolds while Beatrice dismissively remarks that "I had rather hear my dog bark at a crow than a man swear he loves me." For these free agents, marriage is oppressive by nature, a palpable representation of the established social order they enjoy criticising.

8. This interpretation is formed by a mounting case of evidence and different aspects of the text. Although you shouldn't use different examples to demonstrate the exact same point, you can certainly chain together your examples so that they build upon one another and strengthen your argument.

9. As above, you can also collate different quotes or a selection of examples and comment on the range or variation Shakespeare is providing.

PARAGRAPH 3

While the other characters may be amused by Benedick and Beatrice's "merry war," their psychological independence is not sustainable within Messina's hierarchy and marriage becomes a way of containing their chaotic spirits. Beatrice, in particular, is problematic[10] in her failure to fulfil the role of the pious, subservient virgin embodied by her cousin: Leonato warns her that "by my troth, niece, thou wilt never get thee a husband, if thou be so shrewd of thy tongue." In contrast to Hero, who has become acculturated to men speaking on her behalf, Beatrice disrupts the patriarchal power dynamic, commanding conversations.[11] In response to Antonio's suggestion that Hero be ruled by her father in marriage, Beatrice tells her cousin "let him be a handsome fellow, or else make another curtsy, and say, father, as it please me," reframing the conversation as one about female agency and pleasure. The scene where Beatrice is gulled into thinking Benedick loves her represents a departure from her habitual scornful witticism, hinting at the possibility for her to be moulded into a good wife. Here, Hero describes Beatrice as being "self-endeared." Her disdain, far from comical, is depicted as sinful pride and she is forced to confront this new view of herself. Suddenly, her speech breaks into emotive blank verse: "What fire is in mine ears / Can this be true?" Her scornful, proto-feminist façade is abandoned, at least temporarily, along with her prosaic jibes. Nevertheless, Shakespeare does not deprive Beatrice of voice and agency.

10. This hints at the potential audience response; you could even take this a step further and discuss the differences between how an Elizabethan audience and a modern-day one might respond to Beatrice's character, using this to reflect on the extent to which society has changed, or the extent to which the play embodies universal truths.

11. As always, comparing characters will often enable you to make more sophisticated points than merely analysing a character in isolation. This is especially true of *Much Ado* given the prevalence of doubles and symmetry – Shakespeare *wants* audiences to reflect on the similarities and differences between characters and relationships!

After the aborted wedding, her bleak command to Benedick to "kill Claudio" is a strident stand against her society's ingrained misogyny. This forces Benedick to reject chivalric notions of masculine comradery and loyalty to Claudio by challenging him to a duel. Where once he bantered with Claudio almost as a brother, he now spurns his friend's "gossip like humour" and holds him accountable for his callous naïvety.

CONCLUSION

At the play's resolution, marriage is presented as the natural destination, the comic bliss which awaits the noble characters at the conclusion of their trials.[12] Benedick's final words to Beatrice "peace, I will stop your mouth" hint at a rapid sexual and emotional submission on her part. Indeed, the normally garrulous Beatrice remains silent for the remainder of the play, her feisty spirit conquered by the restraints of married life. Don Pedro, however, seems to be deprived of some social power: it is Benedick who declares he will "devise" punishments for the villainous Don John, orders dancing and tells the Prince to "get *thee* a wife!" brazenly using the familiar form. While Shakespeare does not seek to overturn Messina's social structure, this small act of rebellion seems to indicate support for some deviation from rigid class roles.[13]

12. At this point of the essay, we must take the discussion back to the prompt and address the 'to what extent' component of the question.

13. This is a strong, decisive judgement about Shakespeare's message, even though it is presented with more cautious, low modal language; this is perfectly fine, as you are not expected to be completely sure about exactly what Shakespeare meant. Rather, you should take your cues from the play and support *an* interpretation. It is important not to be too apprehensive and make it seem as though you are fence-sitting, but so long as you are able to make authorial intent statements like this (i.e. using Shakespeare's name and an active verb like 'suggests,' 'supports,' 'celebrates,' etc.) then you should still be able to end your essays on a high note.